THE ~~RACE~~ *TRUMP* CARD

Fighting Racism With Trump's Policies, Not BLM Propaganda

MARK BURNS

CHARISMA
HOUSE

Most Charisma Media products are available at special quantity discounts for bulk purchase for sales promotions, premiums, fund-raising, and educational needs. For details, call us at (407) 333-0600 or visit our website at www. charismamedia.com.

THE TRUMP CARD by Mark Burns
Published by Charisma House, an imprint of Charisma Media
600 Rinehart Road, Lake Mary, Florida 32746

Visit the author's website at www.markburns.org.

Cataloging-in-Publication Data is on file with the Library of Congress.
International Standard Book Number: 978-1-63641-131-6
E-book ISBN: 978-1-63641-132-3

The author has made every effort to provide accurate accounts of events, but he acknowledges that others may have different recollections of these events. Every effort also has been made to provide accurate internet addresses at the time of publication, but neither the publisher nor the author assumes any responsibility for errors or for changes that occur after publication. Further, the publisher does not have any control over and does not assume any responsibility for author or third-party websites or their content.

22 23 24 25 26 — 9 8 7 6 5 4 3 2
Printed in the United States of America

I dedicate this book to the American people and hope we the people may see through the Marxist, socialist, anti-American lies and propaganda of groups that call themselves Black Lives Matter. Racism comes from the gates of hell and is wrong despite the color or race of the person saying or performing racist words or acts. Whether you are Black, White, Hispanic, Asian, Native American, or Jewish, it is still racism and evil.

CONTENTS

CONTENTS

ACKNOWLEDGMENTS

I ACKNOWLEDGE THE LORD Jesus Christ as my Lord and Savior. I also want to acknowledge President Donald J. Trump for giving me the platform to inspire Christians to rise up and become more politically active and speak against any political policy that is contrary to the Word of God.

Chapter 1

THE RACIST NARRATIVE— FOLLOW THE MONEY

Prejudice *is when you don't like somebody because they are too fat or skinny, too rich or too poor, too Black or Brown or White.* Racism *is when you seek to alter somebody's future to control their destiny based on the dislike of the color of their skin.*

—Pastor Mark Burns

THERE'S MONEY IN promoting division. Black Lives Matter (BLM) is not about Black people, and it's certainly not about helping the less fortunate. BLM is about the almighty dollar. Again, there is money in division, and for the past three years three major groups have been reaping large dollar amounts by promoting racism and dividing America:

- Black Lives Matter (which I believe has become intertwined with antifa)

- the mainstream media

- liberal Left Democrats (many of whom are essentially Marxists)

BLACK LIVES MATTER MONEY

After George Floyd was killed by police in 2020, BLM gained national attention and quickly raised $90 million.[1] About a quarter of that was spent on "grant funds and other charitable giving," according to The Associated Press. Outside of that we don't know where the money went! We do know that its national president, Patrisse Cullors, stepped down amid allegations that $3.2 million of the amount donated went toward real estate that she purchased for herself, a claim Cullors denies.[2]

In my opinion BLM is really a front for antifa. Three women—Cullors, Alicia Garza, and Opal Tometi—started BLM, and at one point the BLM website said the group wanted to disrupt Western culture. The group utilizes language from Karl Marx himself, with Cullors describing herself and Garza as "trained Marxists."[3] For many BLM activists, the aim is to disrupt American government and dismantle the classes of rich and poor. If the events of the summer of 2020 are any indication, many BLM protesters seem to want to revolutionize American culture by any means necessary, whether through chaos, burning buildings, or disseminating false information.

I will say more about BLM, but for now let's look at how mainstream media is benefiting from the racial division promoted by BLM.

Mainstream Media Money

The mainstream media benefits from the divisive, ugly narrative that fuels racism in America. Violent racial riots sell papers. When police cars are smashed, businesses are looted, and fires are set to homes and businesses, people watch. And the more people watch, the more commercial ads are sold. As more commercial ads are sold, more money is made. People are making money because advertising costs are going up. It's to the point that mainstream media doesn't just report the facts. The media takes bits and pieces of the truth and creates a narrative that will pull in viewers so it can line its pockets.

I equate the division the mainstream media generates among races to going to war. As long as there are two sides fighting, people will watch. I have more to say about mainstream media's money grab, but first I want to help us follow the money being made by liberal Left Democrats.

Liberal Left Democrat Money

Right now the liberal Left controls the mainstream media. Most people listen to the media, and then the media tells them there's massive racism in America. Without question, liberal Left agendas benefit when mainstream media generates news focused on turning united Americans into racist Americans.

Conservatives don't make money from racism. Republicans don't make money off racism. They make money off uniting our nation, growing strong businesses, and making our military stronger. (A stronger military is a stronger America. A stronger America is a safer world. That's a fact.)

George Floyd

The racist narrative is perpetuated in different ways. As long as the media, antifa, and BLM are able to spread racism and fear, their narratives march forward and lead our nation into racial upheaval and violence.

Let's take the story of George Floyd, for example. On May 25, 2020, George Floyd, a forty-six-year-old Black man, was killed in Minneapolis when a White police officer knelt on Floyd's neck while restraining him to handcuff and arrest him. Floyd complained he couldn't breathe, but the officer did not take his knee off his neck, and Floyd died while other officers and civilians stood by watching.[4] What happened that day was terrible and never should have happened. An outcry for justice came from races all over the world, and rightly so.

Having said that, let's be honest, for many years that brother was not a good guy at all. Floyd abused drugs and was arrested several times on charges of theft. His rap sheet shows that he consistently made bad, violent decisions on his own. Neither White people nor the police made him behave that way.

George Floyd had a history of committing violent acts within his own community, among his own people. We don't want to talk about that. As long as we jump on a short video clip without seeing the whole picture, we create the narrative that insists White people are out to kill Black people. That's good for the mainstream media business. It's good for fundraising. It was especially good for BLM and antifa activists, which used this incident to promote violence, looting, and mayhem in our nation's city streets.

FOLLOW THE MONEY—AND THE TV RATINGS

BLM is an organization that gains exponentially from this false narrative, along with the liberal White media—the CNN and MSNBC types. From what I've observed, people don't really watch their shows until they're talking about war, division, and race. I mean, look at the numbers. CNN has half as many prime-time viewers as Fox News, and MSNBC is also trailing far behind Fox News.[5] One of the greatest news stories that these liberal media organizations and newspapers can find is a White cop killing a Black person.

The journalist says, "A bystander captured it on camera."

Oh, this is good news. People will want to buy. People will watch. The liberal advertisers win while weaving this "good news" into their socialist narrative. Ultimately, it's all about getting people to buy their products. It is a cesspool of money.

"Is MSNBC Racist?" I Asked

Many of the journalists at CNN and MSNBC are liberal types, led by White liberal Democrats who don't care about Black Americans as much as getting the racist narrative out there. I remember being on MSNBC's *Morning Joe* show with Rev. Al Sharpton and several others.

Mika Brzezinski had asked me if President Trump was racist, and she and the other hosts ganged up on me to the extent that President Trump later demanded that she apologize to me.[6]

After our on-air exchange, I asked her, "Mika, is MSNBC racist?"

She looked shocked and confused.

I said, "Rev. Al Sharpton had a five-day-a-week show. I don't believe in his policies, but I'm saying you cut his show to one day a week. He used to have a five-day-a-week show. How many other Black people do you have leading or anchoring their own shows? This very popular Black civil rights icon had his daily show pulled by the so-called 'news organization' that is supposed to be about advancing people of color and pointing out those 'racist White bigots, Trump-loving Republicans'? MSNBC uses Black faces just like Democrats, without giving them any real positions."

She looked stunned.

I had my answer: there wasn't one! So don't give me a mouthful of politically correct propaganda. Give me real policies that are going to bring a real change to my life.

DID THE MEDIA REALLY TALK ABOUT PRESIDENT TRUMP'S POLICIES?

When in office, Donald Trump increased the income and financial backing of the historically Black colleges and universities (HBCUs) in this country. The mainstream media gave only brief attention to those policies. There may have been a little blip, but the media didn't want to see a united gathering of historically Black colleges' and universities' professors and presidents in the White House, more specifically in the Oval Office, celebrating President Donald Trump and what he was doing for African Americans' educational institutions.

On the other hand, our first Black president, Barack Obama, was a true liberal. He led an administration of liberal leftists. As difficult as it may be to fathom, their Democratic policies took away funding from HBCUs by allowing a program to expire and unfortunately waited a full year before renewing it—a true disservice to our Black community.[7]

The media also didn't talk much about the prison reform that was passed during Trump's administration, which I'll go into detail about later in this chapter. The media will not point these things out, but it will highlight President Trump saying there were "very fine people on both sides."[8]

WHAT DID THE MEDIA REALLY REPORT ABOUT DONALD TRUMP?

I don't know how many times a White man has to denounce the Ku Klux Klan in order for it to stick.

President Trump denounced white supremacy and

anti-Semitism in a speech on August 14, 2017, soon after a woman was killed at a rally in Charlottesville, Virginia, when violence broke out between white supremacists and counterprotesters. Trump referred to the debate over removing a Robert E. Lee statue, which spawned the rally in Charlottesville, when he said, "You also had people that were very fine people on both sides."[9] He didn't just say there were "very fine people on both sides." He made it very clear that he denounced the KKK, saying, "Racism is evil, and those who cause violence in its name are criminals and thugs, including the KKK, neo-Nazis, white supremacists, and other hate groups that are repugnant to everything we hold dear as Americans."[10]

The mainstream media would not highlight him constantly repeating that he doesn't endorse former KKK leader David Duke, the KKK, or any form of white supremacy. He stated that there is no place for racism in our nation. The media glossed over that and instead focused on the part of the quote where he said there were "very fine people on both sides" and declared Trump a racist.

Yes, there's more that the media selectively did not report regarding the opportunities President Trump created for Black Americans.

They did not highlight how the Trump administration was helping former inmates get and maintain jobs by connecting those former inmates with local churches and nonprofits, such as Big Brothers Big Sisters, that help reintegrate them into society. Even though they may have served stints in prison, they don't have to continue being prisoners of their pasts because they can now get jobs. We are not talking about getting a low-paying job either;

we are talking about former inmates being able to have a career. All this was the result of Trump policies that were essentially glossed over by the media when compared with how much time they spent claiming he was a racist. They didn't even talk about the Opportunity Zones he created and how, even right now, business leaders like me can invest in urban centers in our country that will help create jobs for Black Americans.

Our country has so many abandoned areas, such as in Baltimore, California, and lower parts of South Carolina. Because of President Trump's Opportunity Zones, business leaders are now putting billions of dollars into some of these deserted areas.[11] These resources are to create jobs for people directly affected in these desolate communities.

The liberal media focuses mostly on things that will make President Trump look like a racist, which forces people to choose sides. Again, that creates more division.

Let me emphasize that there's very little integrity in the mainstream media today. As long as there are two sides fighting, people will watch. The liberal media controls what we see on the television screen. It controls the radio broadcasts. It controls the alphabet television networks. It no longer reports the news; it stages the news to get viewers to watch.

CREATING A MODERN-DAY RACIST PEOPLE

The three major groups that are gaining large dollar amounts by promoting racism and dividing America are BLM, the mainstream media, and the liberal Left Democrats. Together they have formed a narrative in an effort to create a modern-day racist people—and I don't mean just White people.

I say it again: BLM has nothing to do with Black lives. BLM is promoting anarchy and racism, and in my opinion its goal is to divide and conquer. In my view BLM and antifa are Marxist movements fueled by a Communist agenda. We should propose a full congressional investigation to see if BLM has any foreign money ties and terrorism connections.

As an aside, the liberal Left Democrats kept talking about the dangers of foreign interference in US elections when it's more likely they were using foreign funds to steal the presidential election in 2020.

In a lot of ways BLM, antifa, the mainstream media, and the liberal Left are forcing White people to choose sides. I know White people right now who have never had a racist bone in their bodies. Now they're having to defend themselves because they are automatically suspected of being racists because of the color of their skin. If they're Republicans, conservative, or supporters of Trump, they are most definitely pegged as racists.

The media has a major role in creating that false narrative. It will continue to build on that narrative because it forces people to be divided and not united.

WHY CRITICAL RACE THEORY IS DANGEROUS

Let's get into critical race theory (CRT) and why it is dangerous. CRT simply is an ideology that states that the institutions of the United States are inherently racist and that every major institution in the United States has a racist agenda.

The truth is that CRT is racist. It's an ideology that will keep people of color from advancing in America. It's almost comical to say it, but according to CRT, you are racist simply for being born White. According to CRT, you can say the legal system and the police force are racist because they are American institutions.

CRT is dangerous because it is teaching hate and division. It's not teaching love and unification. The result of CRT will be the destruction of democracy in this country because, as I stated earlier, if you believe that systems are automatically against you, then you're going to challenge and ultimately revolt against those systems.

That is why many Black men buck or challenge the authority of police. They believe deep down inside that police departments are racist. Actually, it's not that they are racist. Many Black men don't see their actions as the problem. They see the police as their real problem. In many cases it never crosses their minds that they are engaging in illegal activities.

Not all Black men engage in illegal activities, of course. But some of those who do don't think their actions—such as carrying a gun illegally, dealing in prostitution or drugs, or committing violence—are wrong. Rather, they think they are being targeted by the police simply because of the color of their skin.

In their minds it's a fact that the police are racist. Therefore, they think, "I'm not breaking the law. I'm going to challenge the authority of the police *not* because I'm doing something wrong but because they are racist." It's the same concept in the banking systems, federal prisons, and other federal and state systems.

CRT says every institution in the United States is essentially racist. That's what's being taught today. And it is creating resentment in the fabric of America. I believe if it continues, it will ultimately challenge democracy and America as we know it will eventually break down. Why? The reason, as I said earlier, is it will force people to challenge our fundamental institutions, and that, I believe, will ultimately lead to a breakdown of society and a potential civil war within our own nation. In the end liberal Whites are going to realize, "We screwed up. We're supporting Marxist, socialist ideology that is not the red, white, and blue of America."

You already see what happened when the George Floyd protests occurred and brought billions of dollars in damage. Every time a White cop shoots or kills a Black person, the result is damage, anarchy, and violence that often takes place in communities with Black-owned businesses. Destruction prevails. I believe that kind of mentality will spread, not just among Black men who challenge the police (because there aren't enough fathers teaching their sons to respect authority), but it will transfer into the banking system. It will transfer into the housing system. The undercurrent of disrespect will be there.

RACIAL WAR IS GOOD FOR BUSINESS

You can't sell papers with peace. War and division are really good for business—and the current domestic war we are fighting is a war between races.

This is, again, a tactic to force people to draw a line in

the sand. This is happening even with Black people in my own community. There are Black people who had plenty of White friends in their circles before 2020, but now they're being looked at like they are Uncle Toms or sellouts for having one or more White people in their circles. Interracial couples are especially getting the side-eye by those within the Black community. The media is creating those false narratives that people can't get along.

Let me be clear. Racism knows no color. Poverty knows no color. Poverty doesn't care what race you are. There are White poor people right now in Appalachia who don't even have running water. The policies of President Trump were tackling those problems and bringing hope to those Americans. Once again, the mainstream media doesn't want to talk about the Platinum Plan that President Trump was creating. So let me talk about it right now.

TRUMP'S PLATINUM PLAN—A MISSED OPPORTUNITY

I believe Donald Trump will be the Republican presidential nominee in 2024. I believe that when Republicans retake the House and save the Senate in 2022, President Trump will run again, be named our Republican presidential nominee, and become the forty-seventh president of the United States. He can then enact the Platinum Plan.

The Platinum Plan was one of the last policies President Trump developed and was designed to create half a million Black-owned businesses in America. Its purpose was to create an additional three million new jobs for the Black community, increase access to capital in Black communities by almost $500 million, increase home ownership, and enhance financial literacy within the Black community.[12]

Through this plan over half a million new Black-owned businesses in this country would receive proper funding. Billions of dollars would go into Black-owned companies, and business is the backbone of employment. Again, the mainstream media doesn't want to talk about that because it goes against the narrative that President Trump and the Republican Party are "all men, all White," as former First Lady Michelle Obama said,[13] and that they care very little about minorities in America. This ideology offends many White Americans and inflames the division—a division that causes us to go to war with one another. It's a division that focuses on how different we are rather than how similar we are.

As long as we're fighting each other about racial issues, people on both sides will donate money.

It's all a money game.

Chapter 2

BLACK LIVES MATTER OR MARXIST MONEY MATTERS?

Indeed, you won the elections, but I won the count.

—Nicaraguan Dictator Anastasio Somoza

Let's talk about Black Lives Matter. The original movement or organization was hijacked. It didn't have any money. It didn't have any backing. People are less likely to attack Black organizations in today's society, so these hijackers are essentially hiding their true agenda behind Black people. The BLM movement let this happen because the hijackers were behind its funding.

The hijackers of the BLM movement essentially want to bring down America as we know it. I mean, why in the world would participants at a BLM event be burning American flags?[1] What does that have to do with improving the lives of Black people in this country or bringing attention to police brutality?

Police brutality is a major lie. It's a *major* lie. This is another reason this book had to be written. The mainstream media keeps saying over and over again that Black people are in danger from the police. In reality, while Black people are at a higher risk of being killed by police, more White people are shot to death by the police than Black people.[2] That's the truth.

BLM and antifa are both movements that hate capitalism and have Marxist leanings. All you have to do is look at the news to see that BLM is obviously focused on anarchy and is using the race card to divide and conquer America. But why?

BLM Founders Are Trained Marxists

As I stated previously, BLM was started by three Black women, Patrisse Cullors, Alicia Garza, and Opal Tometi. Although all three women are Black, BLM has little to do with Black lives.

The *New York Post* reported that a video surfaced from 2015 in which Cullors said she and her fellow cofounder Garza are "trained Marxists."[3] Cullors spent years under the teachings and indoctrination of Eric Mann, a former leader of a group called the Weathermen, which later became Weather Underground, a domestic terror organization.[4]

At the time of this writing, you could still find Cullors' December 2020 video titled "Am I Marxist?" on YouTube. In this video she laughs at first about people asking her questions about whether she is a Marxist. Then, a few minutes into the video, she admits, "I do believe in Marxism. It's a philosophy I learned early on in my organizing career."[5]

Again, we should request a full congressional investigation into any foreign ties and terrorism connections BLM may have.

What Is Marxism?

Marxism is an ideology or teaching from Karl Marx that states that through revolution all classes will be eliminated to attain a classless society. No more rich people and no more poor people. The goal is to distribute the wealth to all citizens, and it's done through revolution. And as the late Chinese Communist dictator Mao Zedong told his citizens, "A revolution is not a dinner party."[6]

There are certain violent steps that a Marxist is trained to take in order to create chaos that will lead to revolution. Of course, a revolution needs funding. Many believe Communist China and various Communist organizations funneled money to BLM and antifa movements. Why?

I believe Communists saw an opportunity during the COVID-19 pandemic to use BLM and antifa as tools to disrupt and destabilize American culture.

YOU CAN QUOTE ME ON THIS

I wrote a statement that says this:

> The true nature of Black Lives Matter is to disrupt American classes and to disburse wealth equally among all races. BLM has a revolutionary Marxist agenda to delegitimize law enforcement agencies across America, which is the beginning of the destabilization of American society and culture as we know it.

Cullors stepped down from BLM, as I mentioned in the previous chapter, amid allegations that $3.2 million of the $90 million raised for BLM went into her pocket. If you follow the money, you begin to see how much greed and hypocrisy are running the show.

THIS IS NOT A CONSPIRACY THEORY

As I mentioned, BLM fits right into Marxist ideology because BLM delegitimizes law enforcement agencies in the nation. Many BLM activists want to strip away the authority of law enforcement. They are working to chip away at the authority of our local police and inciting disrespect and even violence toward police.

Understand me. Let's say BLM protesters incite another race riot in the street, wielding guns, setting fires, and smashing cars. They might be thinking, "Yeah, you can get four or five of us, but you won't get a hundred of us."

What we see in America today happened during the French Revolution. Destabilization was part of bringing about the revolution.

BLM is just one of the arms being used by Marxists to divide us as a people. They do their best to make people bolder and bolder against police, which makes our communities less safe.

We need more people to speak up and say that they back the police. In some areas of our nation people have put signs up in their front yards that say "We support our police." Good for them! It takes boldness to speak out or even put a sign like that in front of your home, but it is one way to speak up for what you believe and create unity and safer neighborhoods in your own community.

Now, this may surprise you, but you need to know that to some people saying you support police is coded language that means you consider yourself a *patriot* and are a racist. Is that true? Of course not. Even so, that is how people are divided and made to feel they have to choose one side or the other (to support their local police or not) and draw a line in the sand.

WHITE BROTHERS AND SISTERS, HEAR ME

I'm not the majority. I'm a minority among minorities because so many of my Black brothers and sisters have walked away from me. It's so important for my White brothers and sisters to open their mouths and put Satan in his place and kick him in the mouth. Shut him up!

Our nation needs prominent White pastors to speak

up on Sunday mornings and say exactly what needs to be said. Back up those of us who are in a minority. We need more people of every color saying, "We back the police. Make our communities safe."

We Are Being Set Up for Genocide

If we allow these Marxist-backed groups to remove those who keep us safe and strip their power and authority away, then we are setting ourselves up to be just like Nigeria and India, where the police are often extremely corrupt. They literally get away with murder.[7]

Marxist-backed groups would like nothing more than to federalize the police system so they can create military police.

In India, Christians have been beaten and hacked to death; churches have been burned to the ground by Hindus.[8] Women have been burned alive.[9] While visiting India, I was told that in some cases the women's murderers sent out reports saying the community killed them because they had affairs. No; the murderers killed the women because they were Christians. If we take away the authority of police, murder and violence go up.

Minnesota has shown us what happens when rioters burn down cities.[10] What choice would police have but to use force to restore order, which could result in the deaths of protesters? It's so important to support our local police.

COVID-19 and Vaccine Control

Marxists say their goal is to make everyone equal so the government can disburse goods equally to all the people. That is Marxism talk. When you affect the finances among a nation's population, you affect the government. Vaccine mandates force people to choose sides. They're not about COVID; they're about control—which lines up with Marxist theology.

Vaccine mandates are about taking away individuals' freedom to choose. Whether it is someone from antifa or BLM who is going to pull the trigger to destabilize our society, one of them will cross the line first. The goal is to create animosity between people so the government has to do something drastic to put people back in place.

Marxists will stir up a crowd and then force people to choose. They are inciting racism. They want more racists. More specifically, they want more White people to be racists. Now White people are getting scared because of the violence and accusations, and that causes White people to look at Black people differently—with fear instead of friendship.

HOW CAN THE AVERAGE CITIZEN COMBAT THIS?

It's all about organizing, organizing, organizing.

Remember, one of the Marxists' goals is to federalize the police system and create military police. Put a sign in your yard that says "We support our police." Buy a few more signs and give them to your neighbors. Show that as a local community you back your police officers and you are against thugs smashing windows, looting businesses and homes, starting fires, and trespassing on private property—including yours.

If you have someone in your school district who is standing up for the rights of parents and standing up against critical race theory (CRT) being taught in our schools, get behind that person. Help him or her rally more people together. Numbers matter. The government, the news media, and your local schools pay attention to large numbers of parents who say their children will not be taught CRT as truth. Show up at the school board meetings. If there is no parent currently leading in your area, consider leading this yourself or find someone who will.

Do you have a message that needs to go out in your local area? Create a T-shirt. Create yard signs. Organize and bring your message to the city council, school board level, and mayoral level.

If you are savvy with your cell phone, search to see if there is an app like Nextdoor that covers your local community. You don't have to give your full name and address, but sign in and interact with your neighbors there and begin to promote some of these things on that app. For that matter, you can invite people to church and reach out to the hurting in your community. My advice? Jesus said, "Be wise as serpents and harmless as doves" (Matt. 10:16). Chances are there are BLM promoters on that app as well.

MY MEETING WITH AFRICAN AMERICAN MAYORS

Because I'm Black and am in politics now, I convened a meeting with the African American Mayors Association. Mayors from all over the country joined my conference call and discussed their problems.

In my local area, Pickens County, South Carolina, I am finding like-minded people who think school boards are allowing too much government overreach and stripping the rights of parents to oversee the education of their children. What I'm doing is forming a small organization of parents—and we need the numbers. The more numbers you have, the more people listen.

I created a T-shirt. A T-shirt is a great tool to recruit people. Get a message, get a T-shirt, and find ten to twenty captains who will go out and recruit ten team leaders. Ten team leaders will create ten team members. The messaging throughout is the same.

Let's say the message is support the police. In that case, on the mayoral and local city levels you'll want to make sure every person in every elected position is 100 percent in support of the police in your city. It takes one leader to talk to people and say, "I support police," and then hold people accountable.

Right now the move is to pull people off school boards who are not conservatives and are trying to bring CRT into our classrooms. We are actively working to remove those people and bring in people to reset the moral compass to what our Founding Fathers intended.

You can apply this strategy to any subject matter that concerns you and your community. We can't wait for some national leader to come in and save us. Again, what is your goal? Right now we are talking about supporting police and resisting CRT. How can we do that? We can make sure the city council and the local mayor hold true to what we value. We can make sure they hold our beliefs to be true and let our police do their jobs.

I led a coalition of local community and business leaders called Back Our Blue Easley Police Department, raising $10,000, which was used to purchase personalized emergency medical kits for each officer. In doing so, we told the officers, "We back you and we support you." We bought yard signs and T-shirts and worked to unseat council members who want to destabilize our country— and those who are too afraid to speak out and stand up for what's right.

WE NEED FATHERS WHO WILL TEACH THEIR SONS AUTHORITY

Numerous problems in our Black communities are caused by the fact that many of our Black families today don't have fathers in the home.

In January of 2019 some people attempted to break into my tour bus at my office. I pulled out my 9-millimeter, called them out while holding my gun, pointed it at them, and made them lie on the ground. Several of them had drugs on them. When the Easley Police Department showed up in force, I had my gun pointed at these individuals.

The officer said, "Pastor, please lay your weapon down."

As soon as he said that, I immediately complied and laid my weapon down. These events took place at night. I am a Black man and was in a predominantly White community pointing a 9-millimeter gun at individuals who I said were trying to break into my tour bus. I laid my weapon down and stepped away from it. Because I complied with the officer's instructions, I'm alive today to tell you about it.

Do you know why I responded that way? It is because my father and mother, Pastors Otis and Debra Burns, taught me to respect the police. My Black father taught me how to respect and honor the badge.

He would teach me and my siblings by saying, "If a

particular officer challenges your civil liberties, then you document their name and badge number. You document their contact information and report it."

That's the right way to do it. Because we don't have enough fathers in the home, especially Black fathers, children are not being taught how and why laws are to be honored and respected.

BLM and CRT are creating fear. They are challenging the authority of the police officers in this nation because, again, the narrative is that the police system is racist. It doesn't matter if it's a Black cop or a Hispanic cop or an Asian cop or a Native American cop. The system is racist, and we're teaching that to our children.

This is why CRT is dangerous. It's dangerous because it is challenging the law and order of the nation, which keep us safe. The same law and order keep Black people safe within our own communities.

Chapter 3

HOW I FIRST MET DONALD J. TRUMP

*Clearly, Mr. Trump, there is a disconnect between
you, the Republican Party, and the Black community. What will be your plan to bridge that gap?*

—Pastor Mark Burns

IN 2015 I was invited to a private meeting by Darrell Scott, a pastor who had known Trump for about six years.

On the day of the meeting my wife and I were about to cross the street to enter the Trump Tower in New York City. I looked at her and said, "Baby, I feel like something special is going to happen. I don't know what it is, but something special is going to happen."

I MET MY CHRISTIAN HEROES AT THE TRUMP TOWER

We paused and took a selfie in front of Trump Tower, then walked into the luxurious hotel lobby. I can't express my surprise and joy when I saw twenty to twenty-five evangelical Christian leaders who were my heroes all gathered together for this meeting. A handful of Black leaders were there, including me, George Bloomer, Clarence McClendon, and of course Darrell Scott, who invited all of us Black leaders to the meeting. Everybody else was White. I saw Dr. David Jeremiah and Paula White-Cain. Since then she and I have become very close friends. Jentezen Franklin has become a great friend as well. Jan Crouch also was there. (This was the year before she went to be with the Lord.) I saw Kenneth and Gloria Copeland, the Rev. Franklin Graham, and other Christian leaders.

I thought, "Who am I to be among so many of God's generals?"

These were just a few of the great men and women of God that I grew up watching on television. I was more excited about meeting them than I was about meeting Donald Trump. I wanted pictures with all of them!

I was there because of our mutual friend, Darrell Scott,

and because the success of my new Christian television network, NOW Network, caught the eye of Trump. He wanted to meet the young entrepreneur.

I didn't really know a lot about Donald Trump. To be honest, I was just happy to be invited.

How Could I Be Seated Opposite Trump at This Table?

The Christian leaders were led up an elevator and into the famous boardroom, where the names of the guests were placed at the table. I knew I wouldn't have a place card, so I sat down in a chair away from the table. Trump's attorney then, Michael Cohen, struck up a conversation with me, and the next thing I knew, Cohen pulled out the chair directly opposite Trump's chair at the head of the table and said, "Pastor, come here. You sit right here."

I couldn't believe I was sitting directly across the long table from Donald Trump's chair. I was so nervous! How could I be seated at the head of this long table of God's generals?

Just then, Trump walked in with a Bible in his hand and sat down. He said he believed that Christianity was under attack and that Christians no longer had a friend in the White House. For the first thirty-five minutes the ministers around the table discussed with agreement that Trump should run for president and that they would support him.

The Question That Changed My Whole Life

My wife was off to the side taking pictures and recording a video clip, thinking this would be a great memory. I felt I didn't belong there because I didn't consider myself to be as great as everyone sitting at this table. I didn't think I had anything to offer. I was just happy to document being there.

I was silently praying, "Lord, please don't let them ask me a question. I don't want to look stupid!"

All of a sudden, I felt a boldness come over me. I heard the Lord say, "Mark, you belong here. You belong here." I kept hearing it over and over again: "You belong here. I placed you here. I placed you here."

Something special happened at that moment. The Holy Spirit gave me a rush of boldness that I didn't have at the beginning of the meeting. All of a sudden, a question came to my mind. It was a question that changed my whole life. It's the reason I've written this book, seven years later, and why I still serve President Trump's agenda and policies. Even now it's why I'm still on the news. I'm still relevant in many circles in mainstream media. Be it CNN, MSNBC, or Fox News, I'm still being asked my opinion about something because of this one question that I asked.

The one question was this: "Mr. Trump, many of us Black leaders have caught flack just for coming to this meeting. In fact, others were scheduled to come and elected not to come because of the hate they received from our own community. So clearly, Mr. Trump, there is a disconnect between you, the Republican Party, and the Black community. What will be your plan to bridge that gap?"

The room fell silent except for three other Black pastors, who readily agreed with my question.

When I asked Donald Trump that question, he lit up. He leaned forward and said, "That's the very reason why I'm here. This is why I have you leaders here." It's not that he didn't already know the answer, but this was something that would challenge him when he ran for office. I could imagine those who were in the meeting asking themselves, "Who is this? Who in the world is this guy?"

Trump sat up and engaged in dialogue with the Black ministers on how to reach out to the Black community.

That one question dictated the rest of the meeting. For the next two and a half hours, that's pretty much what everyone talked about. Some great ideas were given. Even Dr. Jeremiah, as he prayed over Trump, prayed that God would send a strong African American leader to walk with Donald Trump as he sought the nomination and the presidency.[1]

"Trump Wants to Speak With You"

After the meeting some pastors ran down to get in front of cameras to talk, while others went down the back way so they wouldn't be seen. Me? I'm a country bumpkin from South Carolina. There was free food there, and while everybody was gone, my wife and I stayed and ate. We gathered up a few free Trump bags and Trump napkins. I thought, "You only see things like this in the movies!" We got our collectibles and ate cookies and subs. Michael Cohen came back and said, "Trump wants to speak with you."

All of a sudden, I was asked if I'd be willing to help

Darrell Scott formulate another meeting just with Black pastors and Black leaders. Mr. Trump wanted to dig into our previous conversation even more and have a listening session.

"PASTOR, YOU'RE LIVE ON CNN!"

Because I owned a television network for Black leaders, I could reach out quickly to other pastors. My office created name tags and organized the whole event. Our first event was in Atlanta, and we asked fifty Black leaders to come. We met in the back room of a convention hall. Trump got there late because of his travel schedule, and we didn't get to have that meeting. However, that was the first time I was ever on national television.

He walked into the room where we waited, and he said, "You all follow me."

There was a podium up there, and we followed right behind Trump. When we walked through the doorway, there were a bunch of cameras and reporters and I thought, "What in the world?"

People said, "Pastor, you're live on CNN!"

So we did spend a little bit of time with Donald Trump and then scheduled another meeting at Trump Tower. I used contacts with pastors on my NOW network and this time gathered one hundred leaders. That's the meeting that everyone wrote about.

ONE HUNDRED BLACK LEADERS
MEET WITH CANDIDATE TRUMP

The media paid attention when we brought one hundred Black leaders to Trump Tower. By that time, he'd declared his candidacy and was running for president.[2]

Even though Darrell Scott and I had set up a meeting with some of the nation's greatest Black Christian leaders to meet Republican candidate Donald Trump, some of the Black leaders refused to come. The sad part about that meeting is that after Trump laid out time and money to meet and consult with other business leaders, my Black colleagues couldn't get past the thought that this presidential candidate was racist. Instead of asking Trump about how his administration would create jobs for the Black community, new Black-owned businesses, access to capital, financial literacy, or access to the internet in rural poor Black communities (such as the lower part of South Carolina), the number one question that was asked in several different forms was, "Mr. Trump, are you a racist?"

I whispered to Mr. Trump, "I'm so sorry. This is why my community is in the shape we're in as a whole. We deal with emotionalism and don't focus on our decisions."

No doubt, it's easier to play the victim. If I play the victim, then that takes the focus of my own actions off my decisions and places the focus on what someone did to me. If I take that attitude, then I'm not taking ownership of my choices.

I WAS ON STAGE FOR DONALD
TRUMP, AND HE WASN'T THERE!

When the presidential primary started in my home state of South Carolina, I was asked to speak as a surrogate for Donald Trump at the Faith and Family Presidential Forum being held in February 2016 at Bob Jones University (BJU) in Greenville. Now, I didn't really think anything of that. My office was about ten minutes down the street from BJU, so I assumed that my close proximity to the venue was why I was asked to fill in for Donald Trump and speak there.[3]

"Sure, I'll go and do it," I answered.

The Faith and Family Presidential Forum was the next day, so I had a short time to plan.

I asked Mr. Trump, "So what do you want me to speak on?"

Donald Trump talked about how he's against abortion. He is a pro-lifer now, not a pro-choicer. He also said that Christianity is under attack. Trump said it's easier for Islam and Muslims to enter this country than refugee Christians. He genuinely felt that our religious liberties were being stripped away from us under Democrat Barack Obama's administration.

I was brand new to politics. When I got to the Faith and Family Presidential Forum, I didn't know that so many of the presidential candidates were going to be there. I thought I was just going to speak to a group of people and then leave. But when I arrived, I saw Jeb Bush, Dr. Ben Carson, Sen. Ted Cruz, and Sen. Marco Rubio. The one person I didn't see was Donald Trump. I was there for Donald Trump, and *he wasn't there*! I was his stand-in.

For a split second, I got to feel as if I were a presidential candidate running for the nomination of the Republican Party. When I got on stage, though, I felt the Holy Spirit again. I just began to talk about what Donald Trump told me—how he was pro-life and not pro-choice and how he had professed Jesus Christ as his Lord and Savior. The Lord gave me words in such a way that I felt I had won the crowd over.

That's saying a lot because this was a Ted Cruz audience. This was not a Donald Trump audience. Mr. Trump saw the speech—he watched it live. After leaving the stage, I was asked to speak all over the place. That started my journey of speaking for Donald Trump live on stage and within the media. In the beginning I gave small educational speeches, and that grew to larger things. I started traveling with him and introduced Donald Trump on stage right before he'd come up. That is how it all began.

Chapter 4

TRUMP'S FAITH AND HIS FIGHT FOR BLACK AMERICA AND RELIGIOUS FREEDOM

*Donald Trump professed to me that
Jesus Christ is his Lord and Savior.*

—PASTOR MARK BURNS

MORE THAN TWO decades ago, before Donald Trump ran for president, he received Jesus Christ as his Savior. Pastor Paula White-Cain led Donald Trump to the Lord that day and has since been a dear friend and influential spiritual adviser to him. I want to give a shout-out to Pastor White-Cain because she is the one who brought all those Christian leaders together at Trump Tower, and to this day she is the closest person to President Trump in his spiritual walk with the Lord.

That being said, people sometimes look at President Trump and say, "Oh, he said this or he did that." I hear it all the time. Even in 2024 we will not be voting for the next pastor of the United States. We'll be voting for the *president* of the United States. The president is not our spiritual leader. Your pastor is your spiritual leader. But more importantly, Jesus is your Messiah and Savior if you've received His gift of salvation. God is the One who is on the throne, and the Holy Spirit is your guide. I believe in a three-person God—God the Father, God the Son (Jesus Christ), and God the Holy Spirit. The Bible says of His government, "There will be no end" (Isaiah 9:7). But Donald Trump is not God, nor does he claim to be.

PRESIDENT TRUMP LOVES GOD, HIS FAMILY, AND PEOPLE

It gives me great joy to tell you that Donald Trump professed to me that Jesus Christ is his Lord and Savior. In the years I've known him, I've watched President Trump grow in the Lord. I've watched him pray more. I've watched him be more concerned about people. He just has a love for people—and it is a real love.

These stories don't get reported. The media doesn't talk about this.

President Trump privately grew in the Lord. His marriage grew in the Lord. His children grew in the Lord. Although he has other children, I became closest with Eric, Don Jr., and Ivanka. I talk with them, and I can tell you their love for their father is real. Oh, my Lord, they respect and honor him. The humility they all have for their father is very real. Whereas he may not have been the best husband in the past, he's been an amazing father to all his children. He has professed his faith in the Lord and knows he could not be president without the hand of God.

I was honored to be a member of President Trump's executive council at the White House, and he always sought us out for prayer—always.

He would say, "Please lay your hands on me. I need you to lay your hands on me. I need you. I would prefer to hear from the men and women of God than some of these politicians who are snakes. I need to hear from God."

You can find videos out there of ministers laying hands on him, one of which I recorded myself.[1]

Every time we were at the Eisenhower Executive Office Building, he wanted us to come over to the Oval Office and spend time with him. And we did. There are things that went on behind the scenes that are personal, things that people could not see and the media did not know. I can tell you that he knows he could not have won the 2016 election without the hand of God. He knows, because he has said it with his own mouth, that God was moving in his favor and in his family. He knows that God continues to move in his life and that his servanthood comes through the Holy Spirit.

I remember going over John 8:36 with him one day.

"It says that he whom the Son sets free, Mr. President," I said, "is free indeed. Don't let people focus on your past and what you did in your past. We all have a past, but you've been set free by the blood of the Lamb, Jesus Christ. You don't bring up your past....The blood of the Lamb has washed you clean and washed you whole."

AN EXECUTIVE ORDER FOR RELIGIOUS FREEDOM

One of the first things President Trump did in office—and I was there in the Rose Garden when he did it—was sign the executive order that blocked enforcement of the Johnson Amendment.[2] That amendment was created by then senator Lyndon Baines Johnson at a time when two nonprofit organizations were attacking him in Texas. Basically the Johnson Amendment stated that a nonprofit organization will lose its nonprofit status if it is involved in politics or backing a political candidate.[3]

I explained that the Johnson Amendment essentially silenced preachers who want to preach and support from their pulpits what the president is saying or doing. For years pastors have been afraid that the Internal Revenue Service (IRS) would launch an investigation into them for getting involved in politics.

Out of his own mouth Mr. Trump said, "Christianity is under attack. When I'm elected, Christians again will have a friend in the White House, and I will sign an executive order blocking the Johnson Amendment."[4]

And he did it. After he was elected, President Trump made clear that he opposed students and faculty being blocked from leading prayer at school events. Remember, it was the liberal Democrats who blocked Jesus from being in the mainstream of American life. It was the liberal Democrats who stopped coaches and even students from leading prayer at high school football, baseball, and basketball games. Trump made it clear that prayer should be in the mainstream of American life.

"Merry Christmas!"

Some people think it's elementary to say, "Merry Christmas," but the president made it very clear that during his presidency, Americans could say, "Merry Christmas," and not just, "Happy holidays." Why? Because Christmas is a big part of our heritage in America. The liberal leftists don't like it, but the United States is predominantly a Christian nation. Critical race theory claims that even Christmas is racist! In their attempt to destroy the fabric of America, liberals (for a time) silenced the voice of God in the public square. They want you to say, "Happy holidays."

The mandate to say, "Happy holidays," changed under the leadership of President Trump. Christianity is the heartbeat and soul of this nation. The president understood this, and now we say, "Merry Christmas," to each other again.

Backstage With President Trump

Most of my traveling with Donald Trump occurred during the 2016 campaign. After the election, I was honored to spend a lot of time in the Oval Office, and I was at the White House multiple times for fundraisers and other events.

As I helped him with his campaign, I was a witness to many personal interactions with President Trump that no one would know about. I often saw him demonstrate his love for God, our country, and the American people. I am always very careful about privacy issues, but I will share a moment with you that deeply touched me.

President Trump and I were backstage at a speaking event. I think we were in North Carolina. I was going to speak first, and he was to follow. On this particular day, his plane couldn't land in the small airport because of poor weather conditions. He had to fly further away and drive a longer distance to the event.

I generally would warm up the crowd while waiting for President Trump. In this particular instance, the event was being held in a small arena that would hold about five hundred folks, yet there were about ten thousand more people standing outside. It was hot and jam-packed.

I did what I normally do and spoke to the group. Folks had been sitting there a long time. I was asked to go back up onstage a second time to try to buy some time. I finished the second round and returned backstage. When President Trump arrived, he pulled me to the side and said two things.

First, he said the week before, he canceled a Chicago rally because Bernie Sanders socialists attacked Trump supporters at an event there. There was chaos and violence at the time in Illinois.[5]

Trump asked, "Pastor, do you think that was a good move? Did that help me or hurt me?"

I said, "That was a very good move—that you canceled that rally in Chicago—because it shows leadership. It shows that you care more about the people than you care about your own ego."

The second thing he said to me was, "These people have been here for a long time. Do you think they still want to see me? I hate that they've been here this long."

He was very concerned that the people had been sitting there all that time, waiting for him to arrive, because his plane couldn't land at the nearby airport.

I assured him, "These people love you, and they are anxiously waiting to see you. They are just as excited now as they were five hours ago."

And he said, "Oh, Lord, I hate that they've been sitting in those seats for such a long time."

THE KINDNESS OF DONALD TRUMP

These are just small expressions and acts of kindness. They won't make headline news, but I want to relate this to you here because I want you to see the deep character of a man who cares so much for people. Most of the folks at his events never met him, never shook his hand, never got that close, but the compassion he had toward them was deep and genuine.

The media only shows him getting punched and him punching back, right? I mean, Manny Pacquiao, the famous boxer, is one of the sweetest Christians you'd ever know. He's a soft-spoken, kind person, but the moment he gets in a boxing ring, he's not the sweet, kind, compassionate person. He's a fighter—and one of the best.

As I've gotten to know President Trump personally, I've seen that he's really a kind man. He's a loving man. He loves his children—*loves* his children! He loves people. He loves his wife. He loves helping people who are hurting. That's why he ran for president—simply because he cares for Americans. He doesn't care for just White Americans but all Americans, all human beings.

When I gave the "All Lives Matter" speech at the Republican National Convention in 2016,[6] he said that was the best speech at the whole convention. He honored me with that statement because all lives do matter. That's why he ran—because he loves people, period. It's not about position or prestige or ego. He was already a billionaire. He was already very famous. He was already very rich. He had already reached the pinnacle of success in America. He ran for president because he cares about America and he cares about its citizens.

President Trump's children love him. Not one of his children wrote or said anything nasty about their father. It's because he loves them and they love him. This is the true nature of Trump's character.

I know firsthand that this man really loves God and he loves God's people. I hate it and it angers me when all that is shown in the media is one little snippet of him being verbally attacked and his reaction to being attacked. Again, think of Manny Pacquiao in a boxing ring. Someone is punching him, and he's defending himself. Consider that the next time you see Donald Trump's reaction to being attacked by BLM, antifa, or the liberal media. He's punching back to defend himself and to defend you and me.

How President Trump's Opportunity Zones Policy Impacted Black America

There is a drastic difference between how President Trump's policies impacted Black America and how Democrats' policies impact Black America.

President Trump's policies created wealth within Black communities through the implementation of his Opportunity Zones. I mentioned this earlier, but I want to explain this policy in further detail. According to Public Law No. 115-97, Opportunity Zones are an economic development tool that allow people to invest in distressed areas of the United States. Their purpose is to spur economic growth and job creation in low-income communities while providing tax benefits to investors. These zones were created under the Tax Cuts and Jobs Act of 2017 (Public Law No. 115-97).

US Sen. Tim Scott led his colleagues in asking the Treasury Department and the IRS to modify certain rules of the road for businesses and investors in Opportunity Zones to ensure the strongest possible path forward for economic development within the Black American community.[7] Opportunity Zones encourage investors from all over the world to invest billions into low-income, disenfranchised, at-risk communities.

For example, on September 21, 2020, I organized a conference call on behalf of Aaron Manaigo, managing partner of Global Political Solutions and a liaison to Otumfuo Osei Tutu II, king of the Ashanti kingdom of Ghana; and Mark Meadows, former White House chief of staff to President Donald Trump. In that meeting, we discussed King Otumfuo Osei Tutu II's desire and commitment to invest one hundred million to two hundred million dollars into Opportunity Zones and Black-owned businesses in America.

This Opportunity Zones policy provided tax cuts for American businesses so investors could go into communities they would normally not go into. It would pump in billions of dollars to create greater infrastructures and job opportunities for the people in those communities. The result? Businesses get a tax break. Low-income Black communities flourish. Those zones are all over the country since Trump implemented the Opportunity Zones policy.

Countless jobs are already being created. This is a long-term solution that has the potential to change lives. This is not a bandage or a temporary Democrat-led, all-words-and-no-actions response to a real problem within the Black community. Remember, the employment rate in the Black community was at an all-time high because of President Donald Trump's economic policies.[8] During the Trump administration Black business ownership increased.[9] There were more Black businesses, I believe, because of the policies of President Donald Trump.

TRUMP'S TAX POLICY CREATED JOBS IN THE BLACK COMMUNITY

There's a reason members of the Black business community endorsed President Trump's tax plan early in his run for president. I was at the meeting where this happened. It is because they understood that the tax policy he was presenting would create more jobs within the Black community. They saw this early on. The result of Trump's tax plan is, again, that the Black unemployment rate dropped to a historic low.[10]

Right now we're going back to high numbers of unemployment because of Democratic policies. It's not just COVID-19 that is fostering Black unemployment. No! The Democratic tax policy hurts Black Americans. Obama reduced funding for a minority business development initiative President Richard Nixon implemented.[11] This was a program whose stated goals were to help Black Americans find meaningful employment through job assistance programs and to promote entrepreneurship.[12]

Most people don't know that President Nixon did a lot for the Black community. The Watergate scandal overshadowed it. In the military a number of Black generals were positioned during Richard Nixon's presidency.[13] Many Black businesses, such as automobile dealerships, were created under Nixon. In one of his addresses he stated that he was going to create one hundred Black millionaires.[14] And he attempted to do just that through his Minority Small Business and Capital Ownership Development Program.

Many of these advancements for Black Americans during Nixon's presidency were spearheaded by Robert J. Brown, senior adviser and close friend to Dr. Martin Luther King Jr. and CEO and founder of B&C International. Brown was the first nonfamily member to visit Nelson Mandela at Pollsmoor Prison.[15] It was also Brown, through the Nixon administration, who helped unleash millions of dollars in federal funding for historically Black colleges and universities.[16]

DEMOCRATS OFFER LIP SERVICE

A bipartisan criminal justice bill called the First Step Act was passed by the 115th Congress and signed by President Trump in December of 2018. The First Step Act essentially reforms federal prisons and sentencing laws, which helps reduce the federal inmate population.[17]

President Trump was doing the very same things that Bob Brown did during the Nixon presidency by creating opportunities for Black Americans. He was taking some of those same plans and platforms and injecting them back into American politics.

Joe Biden and the leftist Democratic Party offer nothing but lip service full of false propaganda. They don't have policies that truly help Black folks. They have propaganda to feed the feelings of Black people while Black people remain financially challenged in many ways. We have the lowest median household income in the country,[18] and Black home ownership has declined.[19]

The best interests of Black people are not a priority under Democratic leadership. Democratic candidates talked as if they were supportive of the Black community, but they only wanted the vote of Black people.

I have some Democratic friends right now who are at very high levels in government. They are upset with the liberal Left Democratic Party. I'm not going to mention their names, but they can be seen on television all the time. They understand that Black people are nothing but votes to the Democratic Party.

In fall 2021 the NAACP issued a statement saying it was unhappy with the Biden administration's handling of Haitians at the Texas border.[20] Again, Black people are being used just for votes, and the Democrats are not bringing a real lifestyle change to the Black community. They don't bring change and growth through *policy*. They falsely promise change through *propaganda*, which amounts to bias, emotionalism, and misleading words.

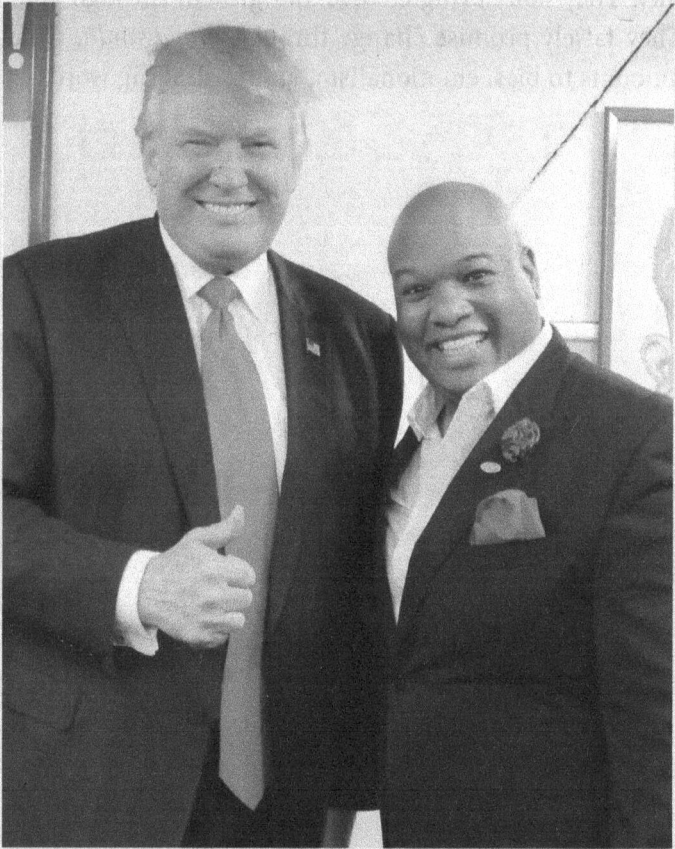

I took this photo in 2015 with then candidate Donald J. Trump inside the USS *Yorktown* (CV-10) in Mount Pleasant, South Carolina. Since 2015 I've had the privilege of getting to know Trump, and I've seen firsthand that he wants America to be great for all Americans, including Black Americans.

President Trump met with evangelical leaders in 2015, and I was honored to be among them (above). We prayed with then candidate Trump during that meeting, and this photo (below) from that moment went viral.

After being at Trump's meeting with evangelical leaders, I helped Pastor Darrell Scott organize two meetings with Black pastors. The second meeting, held at Trump Tower, drew one hundred Black pastors—and a lot of media attention.

Not long after I met Mr. Trump in 2015, I began stumping for the man who would become the forty-fifth president of the United States. This photo was taken in 2016 when I spoke at a Trump rally in Greenville, South Carolina.

I had the privilege of speaking at the 2016 Republican National Convention, where I gave my "All Lives Matter" speech, which went viral.

As I have spoken across the country, I have met so many amazing people who love Donald Trump and this country. I love America and the people of this nation, unlike many liberal Left Democrats.

At this rally in Detroit (above) and throughout the nation (below), the crowds were so fired up for Trump that it's easy to see why Democrats pulled out all the stops to defeat him in 2020.

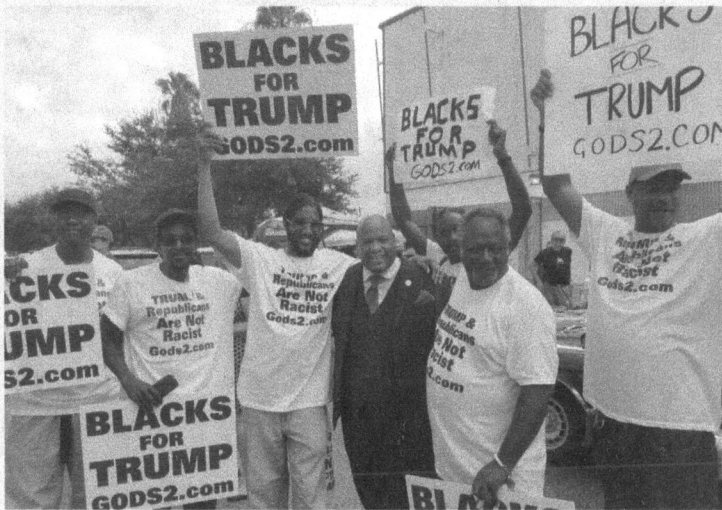

The liberal Left has tried to make President Trump seem like a racist. But I and many other Black Americans have seen through the divisive fake news to support Trump and his vision for America.

I had the pleasure of traveling with Mr. Trump on his plane. I consider President Trump a true friend, and I cherish the cross he gave me during the campaign season.

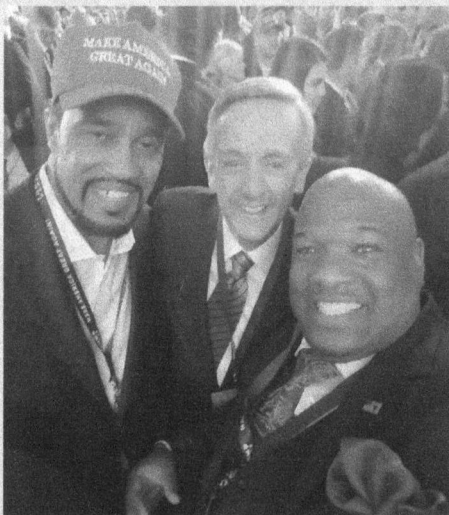

On election night in 2016 I waited for the results with Darrell Scott and Robert Jeffress, two pastors who have become great friends.

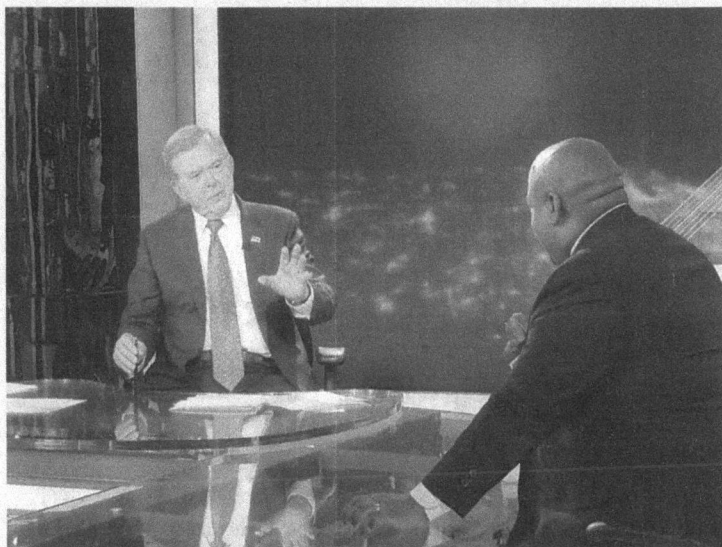

Because of my association with President Trump, I found myself being interviewed by one media outlet after another, including Fox Business' *Lou Dobbs Tonight* (above) and ABC's *Nightline* (below).

On Election Day 2016 I was interviewed by the BBC (above) in New York, where I participated in Trump's watch party at the Hilton, and other media outlets (below). It was clear that the world was watching what would prove to be a historic election.

After he became president, Trump invited several evangelical leaders to serve on an advisory council. In this photo, which I took, we are meeting in the Oval Office, where we prayed for President Trump many times during his presidency.

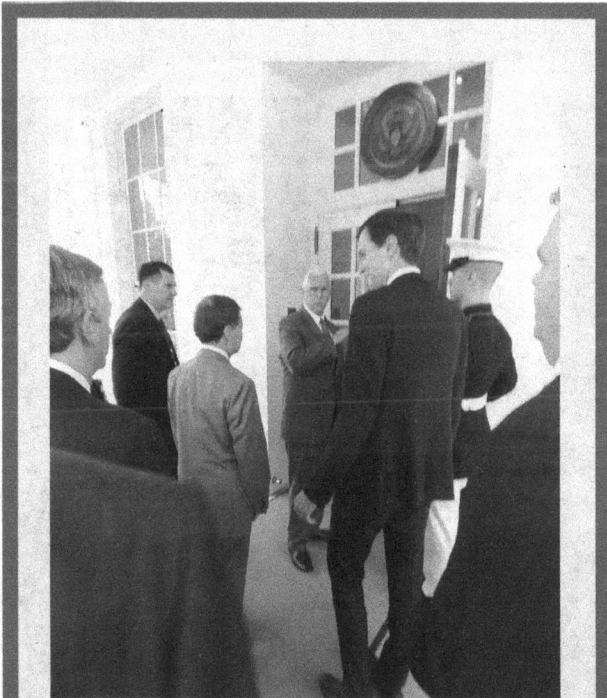

I took this photo while following Vice President Mike Pence and President Trump's son-in-law and political adviser Jared Kushner as they led the president and the Evangelical Executive Council into the West Wing.

In the last several years, I have had the opportunity to meet some incredible people, including Dr. Ben Carson (shown above with his wife, Candy) and Vice President Mike Pence (below).

I got a chance to take a picture with actor Stephen Baldwin during a break from the 2016 presidential debate in Las Vegas.

In recent years I have had the privilege of meeting MyPillow founder and CEO Mike Lindell (above) and General Michael Flynn (left), both of whom have become great friends of mine.

As a pastor my passion is to see God at the center of this nation. At the An Appeal to Heaven rally in South Carolina in January 2021 (below) and at Ralph Reed's Faith and Freedom Coalition conference in North Carolina the following September (above), I called on believers not only to fight policies that are contrary to the Word of God but to rise up in prayer to see revival in this nation. Policies are important, but Jesus Christ is the One who made this nation great in the first place.

I have had the great pleasure of meeting former Republican presidential candidates Ted Cruz (above) and Jeb Bush (below). This photo with Cruz was taken at the Faith and Freedom Coalition's Road to Majority conference in Florida in 2021, at which we both spoke, and this photo with Bush was taken several years ago while we were in Austin, Texas.

At the AMPFest 2020 conference, which American Priority hosted in Miami, I was joined by these great leaders: Alveda King, niece of Dr. Martin Luther King Jr.; and Sarah Huckabee Sanders, President Trump's former press secretary, who is now running for governor of Arkansas.

While in Bengaluru, India, I was invited to meet H. D. Deve Gowda, former prime minister of India.

When I first met Donald Trump, in 2015, I had no idea where the connection would lead. I couldn't have imagined that not only would I speak for him in the media and at campaign events, but I would one day run for office myself as a congressional candidate from the great state of South Carolina. God has opened incredible doors for me, and I am excited to see what He has in store for me and this great nation.

Chapter 5

ATTACKED FOR BEING A BLACK CONSERVATIVE AND TRUMP SUPPORTER

If a Black person calls another Black person a coon, that's no different from a White person calling a Black person a coon or the N-word. It's the same.

—PASTOR MARK BURNS

I HAVE BEEN ATTACKED for being a Black supporter of President Donald J. Trump. Some of the most hateful comments I've ever heard in my life have come from my own Black people. Some of my own people have made racist comments and slurs, calling me a coon and Uncle Tom, or a sellout, a house N-word or house Negro, which is a Black person who is considered a traitor to his own race.

Glass has been knocked out at our office and church facility in South Carolina. I live in a Republican state, but angry people have shown up from all over the country to try to harm me because I speak out as a Black conservative and am a supporter of Donald Trump. I was forced to hire armed security to travel with me because people were so vicious.

I never received this kind of attack from a White person in my life. I was never called so many abusive racial slurs in my life until I was attacked by my own people.

VICIOUSLY AND PUBLICLY BULLIED

I thought my whole life was over after being so viciously and publicly bullied. I've never been attacked like this before, but my desire has always been to champion my community and do it the right way, as civil rights legends Dr. Martin Luther King Jr. and Robert J. Brown did—not in a way that forces people to like or respect you simply because you're Black. No! You will like or respect me because I'm a hard worker, I'm honest, I'm a producer, and I have good character. I'll get opportunities not because of the color of my skin but because I'm the best person to solve your problem.

I side with the great abolitionist Frederick Douglass, who said, and I'm paraphrasing, "I don't want a handout. Just get out of my way. Don't block me."[1]

That's what we need, but that's not what we are getting. Black Lives Matter protests and organizations are causing people to fear Blacks and the Black community. With their actions and words, BLM activists are telling Whites to expect to be beaten down into submission by cancel culture. That's not at all God's will. That's not even love. That's hatred. It's been very challenging among my own people to be a Black conservative, especially a Black Trump supporter—and one who is very close to Trump at that.

I SUFFERED FINANCIALLY

My television network, in the very beginning, suffered significantly. So many Black leaders and pastors quit the network almost overnight.

I didn't know how we were going to make it financially. We suffered. Yet God is faithful. He restored to us literally tenfold from where we were then to where we are right now. God really covered us to where we are completely sold out as a television network. We currently have no time slots available.

That's all because of God!

Has it been challenging? Yes. As part of my calling, I've taken it upon myself to share this message with my brothers and sisters. As long as we keep looking for reasons to be moved by our feelings, as long as we're playing the race card, and as long as we're utilizing the victim mentality, we will not really become prosperous as a people. Never ever! We will not become prosperous as a community until we quit playing the victim card. We're not the only group that was ostracized or segregated due to our race or religion.

STOP PLAYING THE VICTIM

Many groups have felt the sting of racial hatred at different times in our nation's history. Look at Irish Americans and how the Irish community suffered. Italian Americans suffered in the early years of our nation. Asian Americans most definitely suffered at the hands of segregationists and those who didn't want to have anything to do with other races.

We can go on and on and on with this discussion. Groups all over the world have been targeted because of their race. A massive genocide took place in the Armenian community. Of course we know what happened to the Jewish people in Nazi Germany, and the Jewish community is still being attacked today, yet Jewish people are very prosperous. We can't continue to play the race card or the victim card forever because of what took place four hundred years ago when the first Africans were brought to America as slaves.

At some point we have to progress from that. We, again, have to quit forcing people to love us or to like us or to open up an opportunity for us simply because of the color of our skin. Before the Tulsa race riot that took place in 1921, Black people had amazing businesses. They called that part of Tulsa the Black Wall Street.[2] A community in North Carolina was similarly growing in affluence at that time.[3] You should research them. Black people were prosperous because they owned businesses. Now we don't own as much. We spend a lot of money, but we don't own as much.

You Can Be Black and Run a Successful Business

Racism is always going to exist because sin is going to exist. You're never going to completely eliminate racism until Jesus comes back, just as you're never going to eliminate hate. That's what will ultimately end racism in this country—the return of Jesus Christ. Until then, as long as there's sin, there's going to be some form of racism. But Black Americans need to quit playing the victim and using the race card.

Again, I'm a Black man from the Deep South who leads a successful business in the South. I couldn't have done that seventy years ago. It wouldn't have happened. Yet God has brought us a mighty long way, using people such as W. E. B. Du Bois, Marcus Garvey, and Booker T. Washington in the early twentieth century, then Dr. Martin Luther King Jr., Malcolm X, Medgar Evers, and countless others who fought and marched during the civil rights era, including the nonviolent Freedom Riders.

Nonviolent civil rights leaders eventually saw the change they were seeking, as schools and restaurants were integrated. All across this country, people's hearts were changed as Black leaders walked in love and peace.

On the other hand, BLM and antifa protests often become violent. BLM's problem is that it is now entwined with antifa. When BLM first started, I agreed that we need to look at why police treat people of color differently from our White counterparts. According to a Harvard study, a Black American is 3.23 times more likely to be killed by police.[4] Why is that? I think that's a fair, non-political question.

But many times BLM protesters incite fear, making people think that if they don't accept them or meet their demands, their communities will be burned down. That's what's happening today.

SUCCESS DOESN'T COME FROM FORCING PEOPLE TO ACT ON YOUR BEHALF

More American Christians need to recognize, first, that we are citizens of a kingdom. We belong to a kingdom that you can't see. Our loyalty first lies in the kingdom of God. It does not lie in the kingdom of the color of our skin but the kingdom of God.

We don't serve a Black God. We don't serve a White God. We serve the God of Abraham, Isaac, and Jacob, the Alpha and Omega, the Beginning and the End, the Lord of lords, the Lord of hosts. He's coming back again. Jesus is our Messiah. That's whom we serve. We've been grafted into God's family through the blood of Christ. We have to stop playing the race card. We have to stop playing the victim card.

We must realize that our success doesn't come from forcing people to act on our behalf or do what we want. Success comes from hard work and consistently great character.

DR. KING'S VISION FOR BLACK AMERICA VERSUS JOE BIDEN'S

Segregation is evil, and I cannot, as a minister, condone evil.[5]

—MARTIN LUTHER KING JR.

Let's look closely at Martin Luther King Jr.'s vision for Black America versus President Joe Biden's vision for Black America.

Dr. King was nonviolent. He was peaceful. Dr. King stood for unification. He didn't lead an anarchist movement. He led the Montgomery Improvement Association, which was the precursor to the Southern Christian Leadership Conference (SCLC), which Dr. King also led. Through the SCLC, Dr. King worked hand in hand with the National Association for the Advancement of Colored People (NAACP), a civil rights organization formed in 1909 that held the purpose of advancing justice for Black Americans.[6]

Dr. King understood that he had to show America that racial inequality is not just a Black issue; it's an American issue. He knew the only way his vision for Black America would come to pass was for his Black and White brothers and sisters to be unified. He knew Americans had to come together and recognize that segregation impacted everyone and that it was not good for the souls of Americans.

Joe Biden, with his liberal ideology and vision for America, supports Black safe spaces. That brings us back to the whole anti-segregation movement of the fifties and sixties. This national movement really hit the national spotlight after Rosa Parks refused to give up her seat and go sit in the back of the bus. Today, some liberal universities are creating Black-only dorms under the liberal Joe Biden administration.[7] White people can't live in these dorms because Black students say they need a space where they will feel safe on predominantly White campuses. I mean, can you imagine if White students demanded a White-only dorm in today's society? Both are wrong. Segregation based on race is wrong regardless of the color of the person who is calling for or implementing it. Racism is evil regardless of the person involved in it.

We live in a society today that says if you're Black, you can't be racist. Well, that's a lie. That's not true! You are most definitely a racist when you call a person a racial slur. If a Black person calls another Black person a coon, that's no different from a White person calling a Black person a coon or the N-word. It's the same.

Joe Biden's administration is not about advancing Black people. Joe Biden's vision for America does not live up to the dream of Dr. King. It does not live up to the real change that Dr. King fought for when he met with the Kennedy administration and then with the Johnson administration over and over and over until the creation and signing of the Civil Rights Act of 1964 and then the Voting Rights Act of 1965.

President Johnson, who was a Southerner, pushed forward until it happened.[8] That's *real* change. That's not lip service, as Joe Biden's Democratic Party offers today. Today, it's all lip service, and that's what angers me most about the Democratic Party.

President Trump didn't produce lip service. He actually accomplished things. He produced with one hand tied behind his back because he had the mainstream media against him. He had the liberal agenda against him. He had the establishment Republicans against him. He was called a racist every day. Even with those restraints, he got so much accomplished for the Black community in a short time. I am proud to stand behind President Trump and his policies for Black America. And I am proud to be his friend.

Chapter 6

ALL LIVES DO MATTER: LET THE CHURCH SPEAK UP

Love is the only force capable of transforming an enemy into a friend.

—Martin Luther King Jr.

ALL LIVES *DO* matter! Many policies need to be in place to *advance* America rather than *divide* America as it relates to race.

Let me go a step further and say that churches must speak out against racially divisive narratives such as critical race theory, as discussed in chapter 2. Many churches have remained silent. Churches are cowering because they are forgetting that they are first citizens of the kingdom of God. God welcomes children of all colors into His kingdom.

If you are an American Christian, you are a citizen of the United States and a citizen of the kingdom of God. Your allegiance belongs first to God and then second to the United States. We as representatives of the King of kings are obligated to carry out the will of God in every sector of life on earth, including government. Let His will be done on earth as it is in heaven. According to Luke 10:19, God gave us power to tread over serpents and scorpions. He gave us power through the Holy Spirit to conquer any enemy, foreign or domestic, natural or spiritual. The church must speak up.

GOD DOES NOT CALL US TO BE COWARDS

It's not just a good idea to be courageous. The Bible says in Revelation 21:8 that *God is opposed to cowards*!

> But the *cowardly*, unbelieving, abominable, murderers, sexually immoral, sorcerers, idolaters, and all liars shall have their part in the lake which burns with fire and brimstone, which is the second death.

God doesn't need or want a cowardly soldier, yet right now many pastors and Christians are being cowards. Church leaders are being cowards. They are too in love with the color of their skin to be obedient to the voice of the Holy Spirit.

Christians are afraid to be called racist. They would rather appease Black Lives Matter than appease God. That's where we are weak.

Jesus Said Love God and Love People

The Bible says these times would come to pass. Matthew 24:24 says that the very elect would be deceived. It is sad to say that most people today are more afraid of being called racist than of disobeying God's call to unify and love. Jesus preached love.

One day a writer came up to Jesus and asked Him which commandment was the greatest of all. Let's look at Jesus' answer.

> Jesus answered him, "The first of all the commandments is: 'Hear, O Israel, the Lord our God, the Lord is one. And you shall love the Lord your God with all your heart, with all your soul, with all your mind, and with all your strength.' This is the first commandment. And the second, like it, is this: 'You shall love your neighbor as yourself.' There is no other commandment greater than these."
>
> —MARK 12:29–31

Jesus said the greatest gift, the greatest commandment, is to love your God with all your heart, soul, and mind. The second-greatest is to love your neighbor as much as you love yourself. Does that sound like critical race theory to you?

CRITICAL RACE THEORY—HATE OR LOVE?

CRT blames White people for all the problems in the world. CRT says we should defund the police because police are part of a racist system. I've heard parents say their little kindergartners are being told they are racist because their skin is White. If we create a doctrine that challenges the innocence of children and defies the law and order that keep us safe, then we are not following the command of Christ to love.

If a child in elementary school or an adult on the street is my enemy because he or she was born White, then we are casting hate, not love. If we challenge the laws of our land and remove police, who keep law and order, then people of every color will not be safe in their own communities.

Wake up, church!

If you support BLM, an organization that supports killing Black babies,[1] then I want you to think about this: Black lives don't matter when Black babies' lives don't matter. So many churches, especially in the Black community, support the Democratic initiative, the Democratic goal, and the platform that kills babies.

How in the world can you call yourself a child of God and a Christian when you're OK with killing unborn babies?

That's cowardly! And that's why we're losing this fight.

OPEN YOUR MOUTH AND SHARE THE TRUTH

Many in the Christian community talk among ourselves, but we refuse to get on camera and say these things because we don't want to be labeled racists and bigots. That's what happens to White Christians. I think I can speak to this because I'm around conservative leaders (and many of them are White pastors), and we have these conversations about how BLM is wrong. We agree that BLM promotes hate and not the Lord. God has ordained me to be bold. I tell them that the same authority that is in me is in them. Many Christians talk about these things to one another, yet they won't preach this from the pulpit. They get their counsel from the media and don't want to be labeled bigots.

I tell pastors, "*So what* if they call you a racist if you are speaking the truth in love? Your authority comes from the Word of God, not the Democrats or Republicans." We use the Word of God as a guide for how we should be voting and influencing the people we are called to lead. A good shepherd leads his flock. We follow Jesus, the Good Shepherd, not what's popular. Not only is Jesus our Savior; He is our Lord.

I challenge White pastors to speak against BLM. I challenge them to speak against antifa and call it out for what it is—a destructive Marxist movement that wants to disrupt our culture and our country. Don't be intimidated into silence. Speak the truth in love, but it is past time to speak up!

Who will ring the White church bells in today's civil rights movement for Americans to exercise their individual

God-given rights and liberties? During the civil rights movement in the 1960s few in the White Christian church spoke out, and they all should have. They should have been leading the march with Dr. King. Desegregation and equal rights weren't just Black issues; they were American issues. The shepherds of the gospel should have fought right beside civil rights leaders. Then, like today, the church was lying down to an evil ideology straight from the gates of hell that was using fear to intimidate and silence people.

Many Black churches will go with the flow. They don't want to be called Uncle Toms, coons, or sellouts. It's not that they're falling in line with Black Lives Matter—they *fear* BLM. Here's a better choice: fear God, not BLM.

Fear is motivating the corporate society to fall right in line with the doctrine of CRT and the radicalism of BLM. Worse, the church is falling in line because it is afraid to be labeled.

We need people who will open up their mouths and say, "I don't care if you call me a racist! I know what I am, and I know what I'm not! I'm going to preach the Word of God. Love God and love people—all people."

Aren't We Supposed to Love Immigrants?

This leads me to talk about immigration and all the people who are pressing into our borders illegally. Do we love them? Certainly we love them. Do we grant them the right to cross our nation's borders illegally? No.

We've established laws and a process that enables a person born outside the United States to become a citizen of this nation. We are back to law and order. We really need to implement an immigration plan that's going to benefit American citizens and keep them safe. That is not a racist or non-Christian comment. We are either a nation, or we're not a nation. If we're a nation (and we are), we have borders.

While we are to love all people and all people are free to become children of God and members of God's kingdom and government, the United States is a nation on earth, and as a nation we have borders. We need a proper way to allow people to enter our nation without inviting masses of people to come here illegally and not seek proper documentation.

Did you know that Congress never created a proper immigration policy? President Trump had one.

I AM AN AMERICAN AND A PROUD BLACK MAN

Do you understand that when people enter our nation illegally, they are taking jobs from Americans? These jobs are being taken from citizens of this nation, including Hispanic Americans and Asian Americans.

I use those terms for reference, but I'm tired of these titles. I hate that! I hate when people call me African American. I'm an American. There is more to me than the color of my skin. But I am also proud of what my ancestors have overcome. I'm a proud Black man. I have a proud Black heritage from the Deep South of South Carolina. I'm proud of my family. I'm not ashamed of my African heritage at all, nor should you be ashamed if you're a White person.

You should be proud of your heritage. If you are Jewish,

you should be proud of your heritage. Let's get rid of these titles. We need to quit calling ourselves African American, Chinese American, Native American, or Hispanic American and just be Americans.

White people don't go around calling themselves German Americans. They don't refer to themselves as Anglo-Saxon American or European-American. No. Why do minority groups have to keep overidentifying themselves? I think that's more division in and of itself. That's not a policy. I'm just stating my opinion, saying we need to get rid of those titles.

The colors that really matter are red, white, and blue, and after our loyalty to God in heaven, that's where our allegiance belongs.

Back to immigration. In order to properly address American businesses, we have to first address illegal immigration. Thankfully, the Opportunity Zones policy that I mentioned earlier didn't impact just Black communities. It impacted low-income communities of every color.

No More Blame Game

It's important to understand that not every low-income community is a predominantly Black community. Many low-income White communities in America are benefiting from the policies President Donald Trump put in place. In fact, people are being blessed by them even now, in 2022.

Many times when you're poor and broke, you start looking for someone to blame. Providing employment opportunities is about unifying. President Donald Trump was eliminating unemployment through his policies. When everybody is eating, there is no reason to complain about having nothing to eat. There is no reason to blame someone for your poverty or problems based on differences in race or class.

If employment is out there and available to you, then you can't say someone else is the reason you're not successful. You can't say you're not able to eat and access opportunities because of the color of your skin.

Donald Trump was eliminating race-based (and poverty-based) unemployment. That's what eats me up! Our nation is more race conscious with Donald Trump not in office because, once again, people are going back to not having jobs. They are going back to not prospering. Home ownership is dropping under Joe Biden's administration.[2]

POWER NEEDS TO BE PUT BACK IN THE HANDS OF BUSINESSES

The first thing I believe needs to happen is that power needs to be put back into the hands of the businesses. We need to have a smaller government. We can't have a large central government that forces businesses, which are the backbone of this country, to in some cases give up close to 40 percent of their income to the federal government. Tax revenue is being misappropriated, and social programs are creating a "give me" mentality and entitlement. The more the government gives away to people who have a "give me" mentality, the more poverty and less wealth are created.

President Trump's economic policies put power back into the hands of businesses. This didn't impact just the Black community or people of color. All Americans were blessed by pre-COVID-19 wins. *All* Americans were prosperous because of the wisdom and leadership of President Donald Trump, even though he had to fight essentially with one hand tied behind his back.

Chapter 7

PRESIDENT TRUMP'S SUCCESSES AND THE PLAN TO SAVE AMERICA

Anyone who thinks my story is anywhere near over is sadly mistaken.

—President Donald J. Trump

WHEN CAMPAIGNING FOR president in 2016, President Donald J. Trump promised to make America great again, and despite all the media and political obstacles, I believe he delivered on that promise as much as possible in four years.

MAKING AMERICA GREAT AGAIN

President Donald J. Trump accomplished more to benefit the American people than any other first-term president. Essentially, he had a plan to save America, and it began the very first day he was in office. As a nation our successes grew daily because of President Trump. He reversed the backward slide that had been plaguing our beloved and blessed United States. He gave us hope that we can get our country back by restoring our faith in God and returning to our foundational document, the Constitution.

After his swearing in, in 2017, he immediately began making good on his campaign promises. Within a year the world's leaders respected us again. He did this without any new wars. He made historic trade deals and ended the unfair practices that were of little or no benefit to the United States and even encouraged other nations to stand up for their people and make their countries great too.

We had all been burdened with the disastrous Obamacare. Obamacare reduced competition, and competition is the key to lowering the rates of health care. We have to open up the line so people can compete. When there's competition, you bring down the price and you can get really good quality health care without the government interfering. President Trump empowered Americans by greatly expanding health care choice and transparency.

When he took office, President Trump removed many government regulations that had been crippling our industries and institutions over time. We enjoyed tax relief and a tax code that was reformed for the *people's* benefit, not the benefit of big government. Unemployment rates dropped before the COVID-19 pandemic, and those who wanted to work went to work.

President Trump fully enforced our nation's immigration laws despite opposition on every side. We really need to implement an immigration plan that's going to benefit American citizens. Again, that is not a racist or non-Christian comment. We either *are* a nation, or we *are not* a nation.

TRUMP'S SUCCESS STORY

By writing this book, I wanted to highlight some of the great things President Trump has done and is going to do for this nation. This is to remind you that he went to work not just for Black Americans but for *all* Americans.

First of all, he fought for our religious freedom.

Second, he deregulated businesses and gave tax credits where they belong so that more companies will stay in America. His plan is always to produce more products within our country and not depend on foreign trade.

Because of Donald Trump, the overall unemployment rate among all communities and ethnic groups was at a historic low before the pandemic. Trump was and is a businessman, and his business policies kept our nation from being stripped of job opportunities.

As I said earlier, President Trump made people around the world respect us again. He met with North Korean leader Kim Jong-un. Do you remember that they said Trump will lead us to World War III by meeting with the dictator of North Korea? That's not what happened. President Trump brought him to the table! He opened a brand-new door through his effort to bring peace between our nations and freedom to the North Korean people.

The nations laugh at Joe Biden! They don't respect us again. We're not the powerhouse that they saw us as during President Trump's administration. In so many ways, President Trump made America great again, and it will take his leadership to keep America great.

Trump's Plan to Save America

On June 26, 2021, the forty-fifth president of the United States, Donald J. Trump, held a Save America patriotic rally in Wellington, Ohio. The crowd roared as he spoke about how we are one movement, one people, and one nation under God! He said the conservatives of America are part of a commonsense movement and that our fight has only just begun. He proudly talked about respecting our great American flag!

As he neared his conclusion, our forty-fifth president declared: "We will make America powerful again! We will make America wealthy again!"[1]

In the four years that President Trump worked to save America, he laid a solid foundation that only needs to be continued. He already has the plan to save America! It's a good time to remind ourselves that this is our plan too. We are part of it, and as citizens of the United States, we have a responsibility to help make our country great again.

Before I end this chapter, I want to provide you with a

condensed version of the accomplishments of the Trump administration.

TRUMP ADMINISTRATION ACCOMPLISHMENTS[2]

Before the onset of the COVID-19 pandemic, the Trump administration built the world's most prosperous economy. While in office President Trump accomplished the following.

Advanced economic growth by

- delivering a future marked by greater promise and opportunity for all Americans regardless of background,

- increasing manufacturing jobs,

- hitting record stock market numbers,

- rebuilding and investing in rural America, and

- achieving a record-setting economic comeback by refusing to impose blanket lockdowns.

Provided tax relief for the middle class by

- passing nearly two trillion dollars in historic tax relief and reforming the tax code, and

- investing in Opportunity Zones.

Promoted massive deregulation by

- ending the regulatory assault on US businesses and American workers,

- successfully rolling back regulatory overreach, and

- making it possible for Americans to save more and keep more money in their pockets.

Fostered fair and reciprocal trade by

- securing historic trade deals that protected American workers,

- confronting unfair trade practices and putting America first, and

- showing strong support to American farmers.

Promoted energy independence by

- unleashing the potential of America's oil and natural gas, and

- increasing access to the nation's abundant natural resources to become energy independent.

Invested in American workers and their families by

- working to provide affordable, high-quality child care;

- advancing career pathways to good-paying jobs through apprenticeship;

- supporting the economic empowerment of women;

- promoting US leadership in the areas of technology and innovation; and

- championing American jobs for American workers.

Provided a life-saving response to the COVID-19 pandemic by

- restricting travel to the United States from regions of the world with high infection rates;

- repurposing domestic manufacturing facilities to provide critical supplies to frontline workers;

- replenishing medical supplies in the depleted Strategic National Stockpile;

- creating one of the most widespread COVID-19 testing systems in the world;

- pioneering groundbreaking treatment and therapies that helped reduce the mortality rate and save lives;

- bringing "the full power of American medicine and government to produce a safe and effective vaccine in record time";

- ensuring resources were available to the most vulnerable Americans, including residents of nursing homes;

- supporting Americans' safe return to school and work; and

- rescuing the US economy with a historic financial aid package that provided nearly two trillion dollars in relief.

Made great health care accessible to Americans by

- greatly expanding health care choice and transparency, and

- promoting medical research and health care innovation to ensure Americans have access to the best treatment.

Remade the federal judiciary by

- appointing "a historic number of federal judges who will interpret the Constitution as written," and

- appointing three new Supreme Court justices, bringing the Republican-appointed majority on the High Court to 6–3.

Helped make the United States more secure by

- making the nation's southern border more secure,

- fully enforcing the United States' immigration laws,

- protecting America's borders from criminals and terrorists who entered illegally, and

- protecting US workers and taxpayers.

Restored American leadership abroad by

- advancing peace by showing strength,

- renewing our cherished alliance with Israel and taking historic action to advance peace in the Middle East, and

- standing against socialism and communism in the Western Hemisphere.

Rebuilt the military by

- defeating terrorists, holding leaders accountable for bad actions, and bolstering peace throughout the world; and

- addressing gaps in the nation's defense-industrial base, providing necessary updates to improve America's safety.

Served and protected our veterans by

- reforming the Department of Veterans Affairs (VA) to provide better care and improve employee accountability, and

- decreasing veteran homelessness and improving education benefits.

Made communities safer by

- signing landmark criminal justice reform into law;

- supporting America's law enforcement; and

- introducing measures to stem gun violence, hate crimes, and human trafficking.

Cherished life and religious liberty by

- supporting the sanctity of human life and working steadfastly to ensure abortion is not government funded, and

- standing up for religious liberty in America and throughout the world.

Safeguarded the environment by

- securing agreements and signing legislation to protect the environment and preserve the United States' abundant natural resources, and

- spending thirty-eight billion dollars on clean-water infrastructure, supporting seven thousand such projects.

Expanded educational opportunity by

- fighting to ensure all Americans have access to the best education possible,

- promoting technical education,

- reforming and modernizing the education system to promote fairness and restore local control, and

- prioritizing support for historically Black colleges and universities.

Combated the opioid crisis by

- bringing unprecedented attention to the issue and offering support to address the crisis, and

- taking "action to seize illegal drugs and punish those preying on innocent Americans."

AMERICA IS TOO YOUNG TO DIE

Do you like the road that America is on right now? Do you want to see changes that will bring respect back to our nation, our Constitution, and our law enforcement?

America is too young to die. It's time for change. Are you with me?

Chapter 8

THE PASTOR MARK BURNS STORY—LEARNING TO STOP PLAYING THE RACE CARD

*Freedom is a fragile thing and it's never more than
one generation away from extinction.*

—President Ronald Reagan

I WAS BORN IN South Carolina in 1979, and both of my parents, Pastors Otis and Debra Burns, have been great mentors to me. To this day, we serve together in ministry. They are the real deal and were wonderful examples of godliness to me and my two siblings.

CALLED TO PREACH THE GOSPEL

My parents have been married and in ministry for more than forty years. I was fortunate to grow up in a Christian household. At about the age of fifteen, I felt the Lord calling me to preach the gospel. My father told me to follow that guidance and come back in a year.

During that time period, I was a musician, singing the gospel and playing the keyboard in our family group, the Burns Brothers. My father, my grandfather, and all of my aunts and uncles were in the group. We toured and sang gospel music across the country.

A year later, at sixteen, the calling to preach hadn't left me, and that's when I began my official training for the ministry. By the time I was seventeen, I was so honored to be licensed to preach my initial sermon at Mount Pleasant Baptist Church in South Carolina, the church where my father was the pastor.

MY LIFE AS A TEENAGE DAD

My life took a sudden turn when I learned at age seventeen that I would be a father after the first time I had been with someone. I was ashamed and sad. She was fifteen, and my parents said I needed to marry the girl—which is exactly what I did. She was sixteen and I was eighteen when we got married in Georgia. This started my journey of very,

very poor decisions. I needed a house, a job, and transportation—and that's when I learned about Section 8 housing, food stamps, and the Special Supplemental Nutrition Program for Women, Infants, and Children (WIC).

Let me set the record straight—my parents did not raise me this way. They worked very hard and had several jobs. My father was a full-time pastor. He went to college and then became the first Black person dually licensed as a mortician and funeral director in Belton and Anderson, South Carolina. My mother always worked, and we had a good home and lifestyle. They also taught me the value of hard work, which influences me to this day.

I tried to build my new family without a high school diploma, a driver's license, and a car—but I got all those later. I entered Southern Wesleyan University while trying to be a new father who worked full time and went to college full time. Over a period of five years, I went to several different universities seeking to get a degree to better my life for my family. I eventually joined the Army National Guard and spent time at Fort Benning, Georgia, going through basic training and advanced infantry training (AIT). On completion of basic training and AIT, I was assigned to the 4th Battalion, 118th Infantry A Co., a National Guard unit previously located in Fountain Inn, South Carolina, where I trained with the Bradley Fighting Vehicles. I came out of the service in 2006 and started pastoring my first church and preaching the gospel.

While I was getting things accomplished in some areas of my life, other things were not going so well. I was a Christian, but I was making poor decisions. For instance, I got tickets for seatbelt violations, but I had no money to pay the tickets, and my driver's license was suspended.

I went to jail several times for driving under suspension. I was labeled by the Department of Motor Vehicles as a habitual traffic offender. I had several unpaid traffic violation tickets, which piled up, resulting in a suspension of my driver's license. They locked me up, and of course I was so financially challenged (which is a nice way to say I was completely broke) that it would take eight or nine days to get out. I never did drugs. I never drank. I tried to curse before, and it didn't taste good—I just couldn't do that.

I PLAYED THE RACE CARD

I was making poor decisions, and I blamed everybody else. I blamed White people. Playing the race card is really thick in many sectors of the Black community, more than I think most people understand. I thought my problems on the job weren't because I was showing up late to work all the time or not doing my job but because there was a White man in charge and he didn't like me because I was Black. I'm speaking firsthand that this is a mentality many, though not all, of us have in the Black community. Many like to play the victim because we were brought here as slaves and so that gives us some purpose and meaning. This way of thinking, while not healthy, has offered some purpose and meaning by providing a focus that rejects self-responsibility.

Long story short, at that time, my then wife and I broke up before I turned twenty-one. When I got back from the National Guard, we divorced. At that point, I essentially floated until I turned twenty-three.

A Growing Family, a New Start

From twenty-one to twenty-three years of age, I preached at a church that my father and I started called The Harvest in Anderson, South Carolina. My father left and pastored another church.

That's when I met the woman who would one day be my wife—Tomarra. After Tomarra and I married in 2004, I received full custody of the children that I had in my previous marriage, so they came to live with us when they were babies. My wife had two children who were eight and seven when I met her. Later on, Tomarra gave birth to our twins, so we have a total of seven children. *Seven* children! And I praise God for every one of them.

Now I want to back up a little bit and say this to clear the air: During the time when my first child was born, her mom and I were kids. We had a sick child who was born prematurely, and we didn't have any instructions or directions from anybody. I didn't have a job. I didn't have a car. Neither she nor I knew what we were doing. Because we were gullible and ignorant, a family member convinced us that, for our baby's best care, we should sign what is called a termination of parental rights (TPR). We didn't know what that meant. We didn't know what TPR stood for, and they didn't even tell us it meant a termination of parental rights. They told us that it was a way to help us with our child's medical costs and those kinds of things to help her get healthy. That's how it was spelled out to us. Of course, we needed the help—we didn't even have a place to stay. So we lost complete custody of our daughter.

This is where I have a passion for fathers who want to take care of their children. The system is designed to essentially fight good fathers who love their children and who want to be in their children's lives. In many cases vindictive mothers utilize the children as a weapon, and the system often sides with the mother.

Now, years later, I want to say that I didn't raise my daughter, but she is 100 percent in my life today and travels with me. I have a total of seven children in my blended family. Tomarra and I have raised everybody as one family unit.

My Early Call as Pastor Mark Burns

After pastoring The Harvest from 2005 to 2009, I started a new church called Harvest Praise and Worship Center in Easley, South Carolina, from where I currently teach on live cable and satellite television weekly. I wanted a multicultural church because I believe that's what God is. He's not all Black. He's not all White. He's like all of us, and we are all made in His image.

I'm a praise-and-worship leader by heart. I played keyboard in a worship band and directed a choir. I had high-caliber musicians and singers. Praise and worship meant so much to me that I kept *praise and worship* in the title of the church.

I still pastor Harvest Praise and Worship Center, but I also started my own television network called NOW Television Network, which is what actually led me to meet Donald Trump.

The NOW network grew until today it broadcasts into 263 million homes and 83 countries on digital cable television, satellite, Apple TV, the Android app, and ROKU, as well as online at theNOWnetwork.org. As NOW expanded, the finances increased until the business began to undergird the church's outreach into the community.

Harvest Praise and Worship Center established a place in the Easley community for battered women to stay until they can get jobs and get on their feet. The church reaches out to help people at the bottom financially to obtain jobs, change their credit scores, become homeowners, find apartment housing, and even get a car when needed.

Policies I Believe In

We need to go back to where God is the center of this nation. In order for that to happen, we need specific policies in place. It doesn't matter what color or race you are. If you're poor, I want you to be able to be a homeowner. If you're rich, I want you to expand your business so you can hire more people and help our nation prosper. It's not based on the color of your skin or your class in society.

I want Christians in America to have freedom to say, "Hallelujah!" in a restaurant and say, "Merry Christmas," in public without feeling they may offend someone. I will work to take us back to the nation we used to be, where Americans are the good guys and we strive to do right by people, no matter their religious beliefs.

Yes, we have issues, but what nation doesn't? Let's go back to where God is at the center of our nation. Put aside evil ideologies and teachings that are taught to indoctrinate our children's minds. As I mentioned earlier, CRT is the opposite of love. The first and greatest commandment is to love God, and the second is to love our neighbor. (See Matthew 22:37–39.)

We must strengthen our nation and our military against

cyberattacks. Countries such as Iran, China, and Russia are waiting to attack us, looking for a way to destroy and bring down our society. I truly believe that foreign sources are behind BLM and other revolutionary organizations. I believe significant money is coming from Russia and China to disrupt our society with movements such as antifa and BLM.

We have to put the power back into the hands of the businesses so they can create better jobs and better wages. We're giving too much money to the central government. We have to save the Senate in 2022. We must take the House in preparation of Donald Trump coming back and running again to become the forty-seventh president of the United States.

I care about other issues too—America's infrastructure, unemployment, and our natural resources. I will fight for children to have the right to live inside and outside the womb. Our veterans fought to keep America safe, to keep the flag flying, to honor our land of the free and home of the brave. We shouldn't have American soldiers and veterans standing at the back of the line for getting health care. Immigrants who come here illegally are brought to the very front of the line. That should not be happening!

These issues and more are why I've announced my candidacy for the US House of Representatives in my home district in the great state of South Carolina. I believe that South Carolinians want a warrior on Capitol Hill who will fight against the Marxists masquerading as Democrats. I believe American citizens as a whole want someone to stop the Big Tech Marxists from cheating and overthrowing the integrity of our voting polls and election process.

Do you care about these policies? If so, then please join me.

FIGHTING FOR THE AMERICAN REVIVAL

Now, I want to talk to you as a man of God, a pastor of a local church in America and not just a candidate for Congress. We have to bring revival back to this country. The Lord's Prayer was prayed all over this nation the Sunday after 9/11. Churches were packed, and people were praying. Let's look at just one line in the Lord's Prayer:

> Thy kingdom come. Thy will be done, in earth as
> it is in heaven.
>
> —MATTHEW 6:10, KJV

In the Old Testament, Isaiah prophesied that one day Jesus would be born into our world and He would establish the kingdom of God here on earth.

> Of the increase of his government and peace there
> shall be no end.
>
> —ISAIAH 9:7, KJV

The government and kingdom of God will be established here on earth, and not only do I believe that, but I am ready to fight any policies that are contrary to the Word of God. This is a Christian nation.

You can worship whomever you want to worship or not worship at all—that is your right in the Bill of Rights, and that is your right according to the Bible. God doesn't force anybody to become His child.

But I am talking to Christians right now. I want to reawaken the remnant of believers here. It grieves me to see pastors who become politicians and talk less and less about Jesus and the Bible. Policies matter—our government has to function. The border wall is important, overturning *Roe v. Wade* is important, all these issues are important, and I will address them.

But may I tell you that I am speaking out here because the church is entirely too quiet. I will use my voice to reawaken the church until we go back to the days of freedom and faith, back to the days of Billy Graham, Billy Sunday, and the gospel of Jesus Christ being freely preached in this nation. That is what made us great in the first place—Jesus Christ.

Do you care about the American revival? Then please join me.

NOTES

CHAPTER 1

1. Aaron Morrison, "AP Exclusive: Black Lives Matter Opens Up About Its Finances," The Associated Press, February 23, 2021, https://apnews.com/article/black-lives-matter-90-million-finances-8a80cad199f54c0c4b9e74283d27366f.

2. Aaron Morrison, "BLM's Patrisse Cullors to Step Down From Movement Foundation," The Associated Press, May 27, 2021, https://apnews.com/article/ca-state-wire-george-floyd-philanthropy-race-and-ethnicity-0a89ec240a702537a3d89d281789adcf.

3. Jared Ball, "A Short History of Black Lives Matter," The Real News Network, July 23, 2015, https://therealnews.com/pcullors0722blacklives.

4. "The Killing of George Floyd," MPR News, accessed October 28, 2021, https://www.mprnews.org/crime-law-and-justice/killing-of-george-floyd.

5. Mark Joyella, "CNN Drops 68% in Prime as Fox News Channel Crushes Competition in Q2 Cable News Ratings," Forbes, June 29, 2021, https://www.forbes.com/sites/markjoyella/2021/06/29/cnn-drops-68-in-prime-as-fox-news-channel-crushes-competition-in-2q-cable-news-ratings/amp/; Joseph A. Wulfsohn, "CNN Spent Nearly 80% of September Under 1 Million Viewers," Fox News, October 6, 2021, https://www.foxnews.com/media/cnn-september-under-1-million-viewers.

6. Brian Stelter, "Donald Trump: Mika Must Apologize for 'Gang Attack' on Pastor Mark Burns," CNN Money, August 29, 2016, https://money.cnn.com/2016/08/28/media/donald-trump-morning-joe-mika-brzezinski.

7. Michael A. Fletcher, "Obama's Roller-Coaster Relationship With HBCUs," The Undefeated, October 10, 2016, https://theundefeated.com/features/obamas-roller-coaster-relationship-with-hbcus/; Lawrence Ross, "Scold-in-Chief? The Love-Hate Relationship Between HBCUs and President Obama," The Root, May 18, 2016, https://www.theroot.com/scold-in-chief-the-love-hate-relationship-between-hbcu-1790855361.

8. Angie Drobnic Holan, "In Context: Donald Trump's 'Very Fine People on Both Sides' Remarks (Transcript)," PolitiFact, April 26, 2019, https://www.politifact.com/article/2019/apr/26/context-trumps-very-fine-people-both-sides-remarks/.

9. Holan, "In Context: Donald Trump's 'Very Fine People on Both Sides' Remarks (Transcript)."

10. Politico staff, "Full Text: Trump's Statement on White Supremacists in Charlottesville," Politico, August 14, 2017, https://www.politico.com/story/2017/08/14/full-text-trump-comments-white-supremacists-charlottesville-va-transcript-241618.

11. Derek Major, "White House: Opportunity Zones Drew $75 Billion in Two Years," Black Enterprise, August 25, 2020, https://www.blackenterprise.com/white-house-opportunity-zones-drew-75-billion-in-two-years/?test=prebid.

12. "The Platinum Plan," Save America JFC, accessed November 1, 2021, https://cdn.donaldjtrump.com/public-files/press_assets/president-trump-platinum-plan-final-version.pdf.

13. John Bowden, "RNC Chairwoman Pushes Back on Michelle Obama's 'All Men, All White' Comment," The Hill, October 5, 2017, https://thehill.com/blogs/blog-briefing-room/news/354066-rnc-chairwoman-pushes-back-on-michelle-obamas-all-men-all-white.

CHAPTER 2

1. Gina Cook, "DC Protesters Burn American Flag, Chant 'America Was Never Great' on July 4th," NBC Washington, July 4, 2020, https://www.nbcwashington.com/news/local/dc-protesters-burn-american-flag-chant-america-was-never-great-on-july-4th/2352266/.

2. "Number of People Shot to Death by the Police in the United States From 2017 to 2021, by Race," Statista, accessed November 1, 2021, https://www.statista.com/statistics/585152/people-shot-to-death-by-us-police-by-race/; Frank Edwards, Hedwig Lee, and Michael Esposito, "Risk of Being Killed by Police Use of Force in the United States by Age, Race–Ethnicity, and Sex," PNAS 116, no. 34 (August 5, 2019): 16793–16798, https://doi.org/10.1073/pnas.1821204116.

3. Yaron Steinbuch, "Black Lives Matter Co-Founder Describes Herself as 'Trained Marxist,'" New York Post, June 25, 2020, https://nypost.com/2020/06/25/blm-co-founder-describes-herself-as-trained-marxist/; Kat H., "Trained Marxist Patrisse Cullors, Black Lives Matters BLM," YouTube, June 20, 2020, https://www.youtube.com/watch?v=1noLh25FbKI.

4. Jeff Magalif, "Weathermen, Police Scuffle in Cambridge," Harvard Crimson, November 20, 1969, https://www.thecrimson.

com/article/1969/11/20/weathermen-police-scuffle-in-
cambridge-pweathermen/.

5. Patrisse Cullors, "Am I A Marxist? | Patrisse Cullors,"
YouTube, December 14, 2020, https://www.youtube.com/
watch?v=rEp1kxg58kE.

6. "Modern History Sourcebook: Mao Zedong (1893–1976): Report
on an Investigation of the Peasant Movement in Hunan, March
1927," Fordham University, accessed November 1, 2021, https://
sourcebooks.fordham.edu/mod/1927mao.asp.

7. "In Nigeria, Majority of Police Encounters Marked by Bribery,
Difficulty Getting Assistance, Survey Shows," Afrobarometer,
October 16, 2020, https://afrobarometer.org/press/nigeria-
majority-police-encounters-marked-bribery-difficulty-getting-
assistance-survey-shows; Jessie Yeung, "1 in 2 Indians Paid
a Bribe at Least Once in the Past Year, Survey Finds," CNN,
November 27, 2019, https://www.cnn.com/2019/11/27/asia/
india-corruption-bribe-intl-hnk-scli/index.html; Emmanuel
Akinwotu, "Nigeria to Disband Sars Police Unit Accused
of Killings and Brutality," *The Guardian*, October 11, 2020,
https://www.Theguardian.Com/World/2020/Oct/11/Nigeria-To-
Disband-Sars-Police-Unit-Accused-Of-Killings-And-Brutality;
Mohit Rao, "Indian Police Use Violence as a Shortcut to Justice.
It's the Poorest Who Bear the Scars," CNN, accessed November
1, 2021, https://www.cnn.com/2020/12/02/india/police-
brutality-india-dst-intl-hnk/index.html.

8. Rachel Stevenson, "Churches Burnt as Anti-Christian Violence
Hits Eastern India," *The Guardian*, September 1, 2008, https://
www.theguardian.com/world/2008/sep/01/india.religion;
"Christians Face Growing Attacks in Eastern India," The
Associated Press, October 26, 2008, https://www.nbcnews.com/
id/wbna27380721.

9. "India: Christian Woman Killed, the Fifth Victim in
Two Months," Vatican News, July 24, 2020, https://www.
vaticannews.va/en/church/news/2020-07/india-bishop-laments-
killing-of-christian-woman.html.

10. Josh Penrod, C. J. Sinner, and MaryJo Webster, "Buildings
Damaged in Minneapolis, St. Paul After Riots," *Star Tribune*,
July 13, 2020, https://www.startribune.com/minneapolis-
st-paul-buildings-are-damaged-looted-after-george-floyd-
protests-riots/569930671/; Farah Stockman, "They Have Lost
Control: Why Minneapolis Burned," *New York Times*, July 3,
2020, https://www.nytimes.com/2020/07/03/us/minneapolis-
government-george-floyd.html.

CHAPTER 3

1. Mark Silk, "Praying for Trump," Religion News Service, October 2, 2015, https://religionnews.com/2015/10/02/praying-for-trump/.
2. Andrew Rafferty, "Donald Trump Touts Successful Meeting With Black Pastors," NBC News, November 30, 2015, https://www.nbcnews.com/politics/2016-election/trump-black-lives-matter-pressured-pastors-back-endorsement-n471376; M. J. Lee, Eugene Scott, and Tal Kopan, "Trump on Meeting With Black Pastors: 'I Saw Love in That Room,'" CNN, November 30, 2015, https://www. cnn.com/2015/11/28/politics/black-religious-leaders-donald-trump-endorsement/index.html.
3. Rudolph Bell, "Trump, Kasich No-Shows at BJU Presidential Forum," *Greenville News*, February 12, 2016, https://www. greenvilleonline.com/story/news/politics/elections/2016/02/12/trump-kasich-no-shows-bju-presidential-forum/80299020/.

CHAPTER 4

1. Silk, "Praying for Trump"; *Washington Post*, "Faith Leaders Put Hands on Trump and Pray," YouTube, September 1, 2017, https://www.youtube.com/watch?v=a0_mCivoTSs.
2. "President Trump Signs the Executive Order on Promoting Free Speech and Religious Liberty," Facebook, May 4, 2017, https://www.facebook.com/watch/live/?ref=watch_permalink&v=1303862579701472.
3. Robert M. Penna, "The Johnson Amendment: Fact-Checking the Narrative," *Stanford Social Innovation Review*, August 24, 2018, https://ssir.org/articles/entry/the_johnson_amendment_fact_checking_the_narrative.
4. In communication with the author.
5. Jessica Taylor, "Donald Trump Rally in Chicago Canceled Amid Widespread Protests," NPR, March 11, 2016, https://www.npr.org/2016/03/11/470154065/donald-trump-rally-in-chicago-canceled-amid-widespread-protests.
6. Republican National Convention, "Pastor Mark Burns | Full Speech | 2016 Republican National Convention," YouTube, July 21, 2016, https://www.youtube.com/watch?v=pmE6SXpOLhU.
7. "Opportunity Zones," Sen. Tim Scott, accessed November 1, 2021, https://www.scott.senate.gov/opportunityzones.
8. Charisse Jones, "Black Unemployment 2020: African Americans Bear Brunt of Economic Crisis Sparked by the Coronavirus," *USA Today*, June 4, 2020, https://www.usatoday.

com/story/money/2020/06/04/black-unemployment-2020-
joblessness-compounds-anguish-over-brutality/3138521001/.

9. Gene Marks, "African American Businesses Grew 400%—but
They Still Need Investment," *The Guardian*, February 17, 2019,
https://www.theguardian.com/business/2019/feb/17/african-
american-small-business-growth-investment.

10. Jones, "Black Unemployment 2020."

11. "America: Built to Last—Annual Performance Report Fiscal
Year 2011," Minority Business Development Agency, accessed
November 1, 2021, https://archive.mbda.gov/sites/mbda.gov/
files/apr2011.pdf; "The History of the MBDA," Minority
Business Development Agency, accessed November 1, 2021,
https://www.mbda.gov/about/history.

12. "Nixon's Record on Civil Rights," Richard Nixon Foundation,
August 4, 2017, https://www.nixonfoundation.org/2017/08/
nixons-record-civil-rights-2/.

13. Richard A. Hunt, *Melvin Laird and the Foundation of the Post-
Vietnam Military, 1969–1973* (Washington, DC: Office of the
Secretary of Defense, 2015), 536, https://history.defense.gov/
Portals/70/Documents/secretaryofdefense/OSDSeries_Vol7.pdf.

14. Theresa A. Hammond, *A White-Collar Profession: African
American Certified Public Accountants Since 1921* (Chapel Hill,
NC: University of North Carolina Press, 2002), 91.

15. Travis Fain, "Mandela Family Friend From Triad to Attend
Funeral," *Greensboro News & Record*, December 8, 2013,
https://greensboro.com/news/local_news/mandela-family-
friend-from-triad-to-attend-funeral/article_a5e4cbaa-d8d7-
5ed0-9ec5-a78ff9409c61.html; Art Harris, "The Man Who
Aided Mandela," *Washington Post*, June 30, 1990, https://www.
washingtonpost.com/archive/lifestyle/1990/06/30/the-man-
who-aided-mandela/fbd0d5bb-73b2-4b9d-9597-426a4d12acd0/.

16. Frank Gannon and Jonathan Movrodis, "Project: Oral History
Robert J. Brown Part 1 of 2," Richard Nixon Foundation,
March 14, 2019, https://www.nixonfoundation.org/wp-content/
uploads/2019/06/Robert-Brown-1.pdf.

17. "An Overview of the First Step Act," Bureau of Prisons, accessed
October 28, 2021, https://www.bop.gov/inmates/fsa/overview.jsp.

18. "Racial Disparities in Income and Poverty Remain Largely
Unchanged Amid Strong Income Growth in 2019," Economic
Policy Institute, September 16, 2020, https://www.epi.org/
blog/racial-disparities-in-income-and-poverty-remain-largely-
unchanged-amid-strong-income-growth-in-2019/.

19. Broderick Johnson, "The Future for Economic Equity," Covington & Burling, November 9, 2020, https://www.globalpolicywatch.com/2020/11/the-future-for-economic-equity/.

20. "NAACP President and CEO, Derrick Johnson, and Executive Director of BAJI, Nana Gyamfi, Release Statement After Meeting With White House on Haitian Migrants at the U.S. Border," NAACP, September 23, 2021, https://naacp.org/articles/naacp-president-and-ceo-derrick-johnson-and-executive-director-baji-nana-gyamfi-release.

CHAPTER 5

1. "(1865) Frederick Douglass, 'What the Black Man Wants,'" BlackPast, March 15, 2012, https://www.blackpast.org/african-american-history/1865-frederick-douglass-what-black-man-wants/.

2. "The Attack on Greenwood," Tulsa Historical Society, accessed October 28, 2021, https://www.tulsahistory.org/exhibit/1921-tulsa-race-massacre/.

3. "Durham Black Wall Street," Soul of America, accessed November 1, 2021, https://www.soulofamerica.com/us-cities/durham/durham-black-wall-street/.

4. "Black People More Than Three Times as Likely as White People to Be Killed During a Police Encounter," Harvard T. H. Chan School of Public Health, June 24, 2020, https://www.hsph.harvard.edu/news/hsph-in-the-news/blacks-whites-police-deaths-disparity/.

5. Tom Johnson, "The Rev. King Is Boycott Boss," *Montgomery Advertiser*, January 19, 1956, https://cdm16044.contentdm.oclc.org/digital/collection/p4017coll2/id/6425.

6. "Montgomery Improvement Association (MIA)," The Martin Luther King, Jr. Research and Education Institute, accessed October 28, 2021, https://kinginstitute.stanford.edu/encyclopedia/montgomery-improvement-association-mia.

7. Derek Major, "Western Washington University Implements Segregated Black-Only Student Housing," Black Enterprise, September 28, 2021, https://www.blackenterprise.com/western-washington-university-implements-segregated-black-only-student-housing/.

8. Ted Gittinger and Allen Fisher, "LBJ Champions the Civil Rights Act of 1964," *National Archives* 36, no. 2 (Summer 2004), https://www.archives.gov/publications/prologue/2004/summer/civil-rights-act-1.html.

CHAPTER 6

1. "#AllHandsOnDeckTX!," Black Lives Matter, September 3, 2021, https://blacklivesmatter.com/ allhandsondecktx/?__cf_chl_jschl_tk__=pmd_ zPDjA2NtVWr3Y1OsiWxVEGUHPHuRvYxZ8s2_bHAyUD8- 1635019744-0-gqNtZGzNAmWjcnBszQkR.
2. "Quarterly Residential Vacancies and Homeownership, Second Quarter 2021," Census Bureau, July 27, 2021, https://www. census.gov/housing/hvs/files/currenthvspress.pdf.

CHAPTER 7

1. "Former President Trump Holds Rally in Ohio," CSPAN, June 26, 2021, https://www.c-span.org/video/?512874-1/president-trump-holds-rally-ohio.
2. "Trump Administration Accomplishments," White House, accessed October 31, 2021, https://trumpwhitehouse.archives. gov/ trump-administration-accomplishments/.